W9-CHR-711

Visio Services Quick Guide

Using Visio with Sharepoint 2013 and Office 365

Sahil Malik
Srini Sistla

Apress®

Visio Services Quick Guide: Using Visio with Sharepoint 2013 and Office 365

ISBN-13 (pbk): 978-1-4842-0869-4

ISBN-13 (electronic): 978-1-4842-0868-7

Managing Director: Welmoed Spahr
Lead Editor: Gwenan Spearing
Editorial Board: Steve Anglin, Mark Beckner, Ewan Buckingham, Gary Cornell, Louise Corrigan, Jim DeWolf, Jonathan Gennick, Robert Hutchinson, Michelle Lowman, James Markham, Matthew Moodie, Jeff Olson, Jeffrey Pepper, Douglas Pundick, Ben Renow-Clarke, Dominic Shakeshaft, Gwenan Spearing, Matt Wade, Steve Weiss
Coordinating Editor: Christine Ricketts
Copy Editor: Laura Lawrie
Compositor: SPi Global
Indexer: SPi Global
Artist: SPi Global
Cover Designer: Anna Ishchenko

Distributed to the book trade worldwide by Springer Science+Business Media New York, 233 Spring Street, 6th Floor, New York, NY 10013. Phone 1-800-SPRINGER, fax (201) 348-4505, e-mail orders-ny@springer-sbm.com, or visit www.springeronline.com. Apress Media, LLC is a California LLC and the sole member (owner) is Springer Science + Business Media Finance Inc (SSBM Finance Inc). SSBM Finance Inc is a **Delaware** corporation.

For information on translations, please e-mail rights@apress.com, or visit www.apress.com.

Apress and friends of ED books may be purchased in bulk for academic, corporate, or promotional use. eBook versions and licenses are also available for most titles. For more information, reference our Special Bulk Sales–eBook Licensing web page at www.apress.com/bulk-sales.

Any source code or other supplementary material referenced by the author in this text is available to readers at www.apress.com. For detailed information about how to locate your book's source code, go to www.apress.com/source-code/.

I would like to dedicate this book to entire SharePoint Developer Community.

—Srini Sistla

Contents at a Glance

Contents

About the Authors

Sahil Malik, the founder and principal of Winsmarts.com, has been a Microsoft MVP and INETA Speaker for the past 10 years. He has authored many books and numerous articles in the .NET and SharePoint space. Sahil has architected and delivered SharePoint based solutions for extremely high profile clients and talks at conferences internationally. Sahil has authored two books for Apress on SharePoint 2010.

Srini Sistla is a Microsoft Certified Technology Specialist and INETA speaker with over 15 years of experience in designing and implementing IT solutions on a variety of platforms and domains. Srini has authored several books on SharePoint 2010/2013 and has solid experience in building highly customized windows and web-based applications. His strength and expertise in SharePoint includes BI, ECM, Apps, Workflows and CSOM. Srini is an active blogger, contributor on TechNet and profound speaker in several regional user groups and local conferences. Srini is currently working as SharePoint Architect and Consultant, and hails from Washington DC metro area.

Acknowledgments

This is my fourth book with Apress and I would like to thank them for giving me opportunity, trust and support. I would like to also thank my co-author Sahil, reviewers and content editors of this book. Finally, my family who have been always supportive in my ventures.

—Srini Sistla

CHAPTER 1

▓ ▓ ▓

Introduction and Background

You've probably heard that a picture is worth 1,000 words, and also that actions speak louder than words. If you put those two axioms together, you get the idea of Visio. It is often far easier to understand and simpler to explain a concept, a theory, or even a story by presenting actions visually in blocks and diagrams rather than words. Visio is a very powerful vector graphic tool you can use for exactly that, and Visio Services lets you bring your Visio diagrams to life. In this chapter, we'll have a brief background on Visio, and what Visio Services can do.

First, let's take a quick look at what we'll cover in the rest of this book.

What Will You Learn?

This book introduces you to Visio Services and discusses using Visio with SharePoint 2013. If you're familiar with Visio 2010, a few concepts might be redundant. You might want to either skip them or flick through them quickly, or, for a quick overview of what's new in Visio Services 2013, see the Appendix.

By the end of this book, you'll learn about:

- The essentials of Visio Services

- Setting up Visio Services on SharePoint 2013

- Publishing a basic Visio diagram to SharePoint

- Connecting a Visio diagram to:

  - A SharePoint List

  - SQL Server with and without Secure Store Services

  - Data using a custom data provider (using Visual Studio and WCF)

  - Workflows and Visio with SharePoint Designer 2013

- Management of Visio Services using Central Administration (CA)

- Management of Visio Services using Windows PowerShell

- What's new in Visio Services in SharePoint 2013 (see Appendix)

1

Prerequisites

To be able to use this book successfully, you'll need the following software:

- SharePoint Server 2013 Enterprise Edition

- SQL Server 2008 R2 / SQL Server 2008 / SQL Server 2012 (x86 or x64)

- Visio Client—2013 Professional or 2010 Professional or 2010 Ultimate

- SharePoint Designer 2013, available for download at `http://www.microsoft.com/en-us/download/details.aspx?id=35491`

- Visual Studio 2012 or 2013 Professional Edition, trial version available for download at `http://www.visualstudio.com/downloads/download-visual-studio-vs`

- If you'd prefer using the Express editions of Visual Studio and SQL Server, you can download them from `www.microsoft.com/express/`

Why Visio?

Let me walk you through a small story called "My day begins with . . . . I wake up early in the morning, get ready, and start from home at about 7:15AM. On my way driving to the office, I stop by the nearest coffee shop to pick up my morning beverage. I choose hot chocolate and head for the office—yet another decision to make, whether or not take the freeway. I quickly look over my shoulder and as there's not a lot of traffic, I choose to drive on local streets. At 8:45AM, I arrive at the office.

Notice the words in my little story. It's all about initiation, actions, decisions, and concluding. Well, of course these four elements and maybe a few others are required to run our lives and, in fact, any job, too. Simply put, if I want to tell my story in the form of diagram or a flow chart, it becomes a sort of storyboard—a logical sequence of boxes connected together, as shown in Figure 1-1.

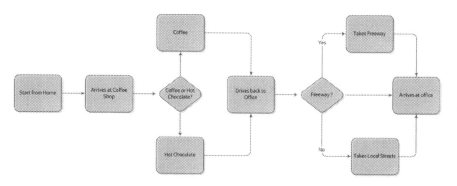

Figure 1-1. *"My day begins with . . ." storyboard*

With Visio you can create a wide range of diagrams easily with the help of inbuilt shapes, stencils, and templates. The diagram scope can encompass the simple, like my storyboard, or the complex, like the network representation of an entire organizational infrastructure. It can target various audiences, from business analyst to a developer to a solutions architect. A construction engineer or an interior designer can create a floor plan. An electrical engineer can create a basic electrical circuit or a logic diagram. There are endless possibilities using Visio; you just need to focus your imagination on the available templates to create your own diagrams.

Why Visio Services?

Now, what if your Visio diagrams could come to life? What if you could power these diagrams with data and share them with your colleagues?

Let me give you a real-time example. As an architect in the organization where I work, I'm often asked to give introductory sessions to many people on the project team, and I typically use a Visio diagram to explain the project details. Whenever there are enhancements, updates, or changes to the project, I have to redo my Visio diagram and present it to the team.

Instead of calling for another meeting, I could update and e-mail a new version of the Visio diagram and get final approval. But not everyone has Visio installed. Moreover, where does this information end up? E-mails! Or maybe in yet another set of printed documents that will just collect dust on the shelf. What's missing here?

1. Collaboration

2. Easy viewing. For a Visio diagram you need either the Visio client and related licenses, or at least a Visio viewer (there's a free viewer available at http://www.microsoft.com/en-us/download/details.aspx?id=35811)

3. Instant update of the diagrams

4. Data connectivity

You've all probably thought at some point, wouldn't it be great to be able to share a Visio diagram that's connected to data, in which the diagram updates automatically when the data changes? And wouldn't it be wonderful to be able to have end users view the diagram in their browsers, without having to install the actual Visio client?

Well, those scenarios are possible. With Visio Services in SharePoint 2013, you can publish Visio diagrams to SharePoint, drive them with real-time data, and share them easily without installing Visio client—all of this by using Visio Services in SharePoint 2013.

Visio Services was introduced in the previous version of SharePoint (2010) as a SharePoint Server service application. These services are available as part of the Enterprise Client Access License (CAL) and they provide a platform where users can share the Visio diagrams using the SharePoint infrastructure. Visio Services provide various data connectivity models to drive Visio diagrams with data, both real-time and historic. Most of the features discussed in this book apply to both on-premises and in the cloud—Office 365 SharePoint Online. Unless otherwise mentioned, the examples discussed will work on both platforms.

Summary

In this introduction chapter, you have seen what you will be learning in this book and why you need Visio, as well as the benefits of Visio Services.

What's Next?

In the next chapter, you will learn about configuring Visio Services, and understanding its architecture and features.

CHAPTER 2

![]

Presenting Visio Services

This chapter will get you set up with Visio Services on SharePoint 2013. We'll also look at the features available and take a look at the underlying architecture.

Setting up Visio Services

Setting up Visio Services is quite simple, requiring just few basic steps. Before beginning, however, ensure that you have Farm Administrator privileges.

There are two approaches. In the first, in SharePoint 2013, simply go to Central Administration ➤ Configuration Wizards and launch the Farm Configuration wizard, as shown in Figure 2-1.

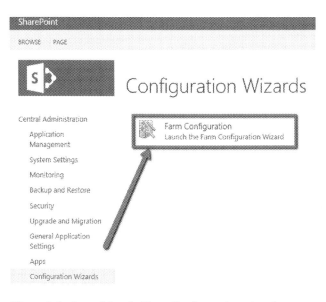

Figure 2-1. Launching the Farm Configuration wizard

▓ **Tip** If you are installing SharePoint for the first time, you'll be prompted to run this step toward the end of the installation. If you prefer, you can just skip it for now and run it later.

In the subsequent screen, you are prompted to 'Start the Wizard,' as shown in Figure 2-2.

How do you want to configure your SharePoint farm?

This wizard will help with the initial configuration of your SharePoint farm. You can select the services to use in this farm and create your first site.

You can launch this wizard again from the Configuration Wizards page in the Central Administration site.

Yes, walk me through the configuration of my farm using this wizard.

Start the Wizard

No, I will configure everything myself.

Cancel

Figure 2-2. Choosing to configure the farm using the wizard

To set up the services, you need to have a service account and choose required services from the wizard (Figure 2-3). Be sure you have Visio Graphics Service checked. If this is a fresh installation, this option will be enabled.

☑ **User Profile Service Application**
Adds support for My Sites, Profiles pages, Social Tagging and other social computing features. Some of the features offered by this service require Search Service Application and Managed Metadata Services to be provisioned.
Learn about security implications related to this option

☑ **Visio Graphics Service**
Enables viewing and refreshing of Visio Web Drawings.

☑ **Word Automation Services**
Provides a framework for performing automated document conversions.

☑ **Work Management Service Application**
This service provides task aggregation across work management systems.

☑ **Workflow Service Application**

Figure 2-3. Select the desired services using the Farm Configuration wizard

Click Next. SharePoint will provision all services selected in this step, and prompts to create a new site collection with the selected services. You cannot choose a service that's already installed because it will be disabled, as shown in Figure 2-3.

▓ **Note** With this default mode and the service application already available to the default web application, you can now create a site collection using one of the available templates.

This approach is very direct. Things get a little more interesting when you haven't set up the services during installation or if you later upgrade your licensing model. In such situations, you can set up Visio Services using the following approach.

Go to Application Management ➤ Service Applications ➤ Manage Service Applications. Click the New button on the ribbon and then choose Visio Graphics Service. Provide a valid application name, and choose or create a new application pool under which this service application will run. As you create the application pool, you'll have the option to use any already configured service accounts or to register a new managed account, as shown in Figure 2-4.

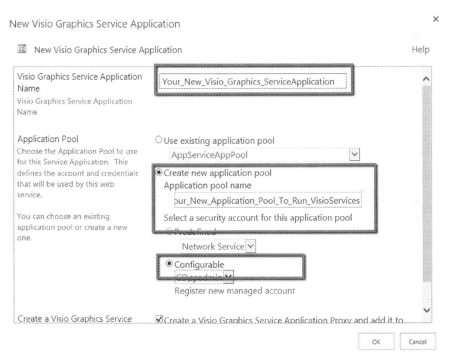

Figure 2-4. Setting up a new Visio Graphics Service application

Your new service application will now appear in the list of available service applications and you can configure it, as we'll discuss later in this chapter.

▓ **Note**   Once you create the new service application, you have to associate it with a web application. You can associate a new service application with a new web application or existing web application.

To associate a new service application with a web application, on the Central Administration go to Application Management ➤ Service Applications ➤ Configure service application associations and select the Web application you want to associate the service with. For the Configure service application association connections option, choose Custom. Select the desired custom service application and click on OK.

Let's now look at an example and see how to perform basic operations using Visio and Visio Services in SharePoint 2013.

Publishing a Basic Visio Diagram

In this example, we create a basic Visio diagram, and save and publish it to SharePoint. The published diagram can then be opened in the browser.

| PROBLEM CASE |

Check the status of five major airline carriers at the airport using a Visio diagram that's been published to SharePoint using Visio Services 2013.

Solution

Open Visio 2013 and choose Directional Map Shapes 3D (US Units) from the available diagrams, and add Airport to the page. Add a few images or shapes, such as Store 1, Tree, and Roof 1 from Directional Map Shapes 3D, and an Airplane from More Shapes ➤ Visio Extras ➤ Symbols (US units) ➤ Airport as shown in Figure 2-5.

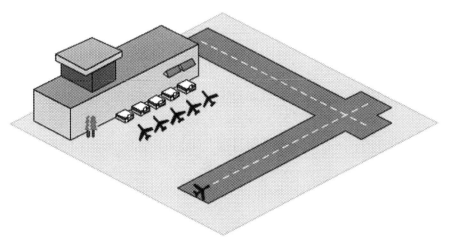

Figure 2-5. *Airport stencil with various shapes*

Your diagram doesn't need to look exactly like this. This example is only for your reference. You can design your own use case and try the concepts mentioned in the following example.

On the File menu, click on Save and save the drawing to a local file location as a Visio Drawing, airport.vsdx in this example.

▓ **Note** Unlike SharePoint 2010, where you need to save the .vsd file as web drawing file (.vdw) in order to view it on browser in SharePoint site, Visio 2013 offers a single drawing file extension (.vsdx) that you can use directly in SharePoint 2013.

To run Visio drawing (.vsdx) files, make sure that SharePoint Server Enterprise Site Collection Features feature is activated. You'll find this on the Site Collection Features under the Site Collection Administration of your web application.

Close Visio diagram and return to the folder where you saved the <filename>.vsdx

Open your SharePoint site, click on the site gear icon and choose the link 'Add an app' as shown in Figure 2-6.

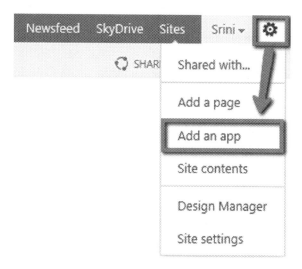

Figure 2-6. *Add an app in SharePoint 2013*

Click on the 'Document Library' icon from either the Noteworthy or Apps you can add section, as shown in Figure 2-7.

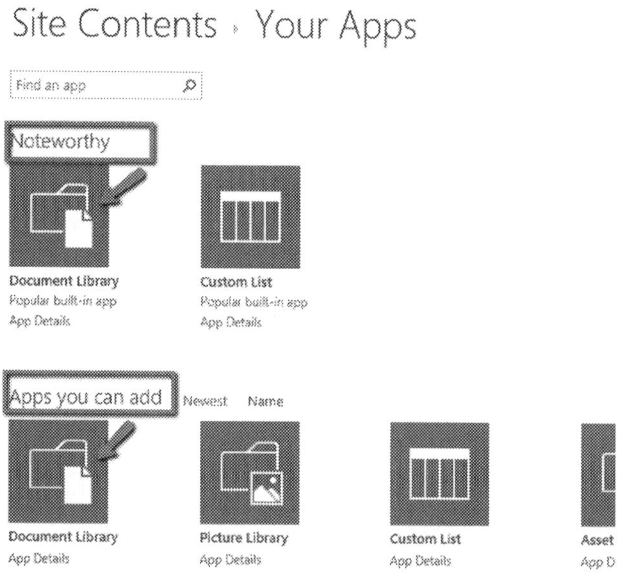

Site Contents › Your Apps

Find an app

Noteworthy

Document Library
Popular built-in app
App Details

Custom List
Popular built-in app
App Details

Apps you can add   Newest   Name

Document Library
App Details

Picture Library
App Details

Custom List
App Details

Asset
App D

Figure 2-7. *Adding specific app in SharePoint 2013*

In the 'Adding Document Library' dialog, enter the name 'Visio Library' and click Create as shown in Figure 2-8. You do not need to use Advanced Options in this case.

Figure 2-8. *Adding Document Library*

Open the newly created document library and click on the 'new document' link or from the ribbon use the 'Upload document' option under the New section. Choose the .vsdx file you created earlier in the chapter and click 'OK'.

After the document is successfully uploaded, you'll be returned to the document library, where you'll see a new item—the document you just uploaded—as shown in Figure 2-9.

⊕ new document or drag files here

All Documents •••   Find a file   🔍

✓	🗋	Name	Modified	Modified By
	📄	Airport ✕ •••	A few seconds ago	☐ Srini

Figure 2-9. *Document Library in SharePoint 2013*

Click on the document Name column to open the Visio diagram in full screen mode in the browser, as shown in Figure 2-10.

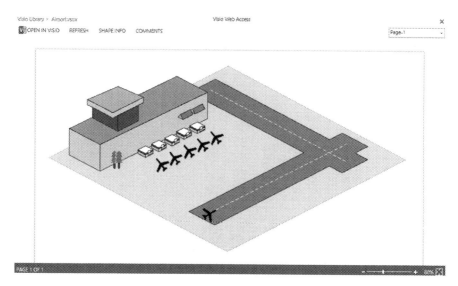

Figure 2-10. *Visio web drawing file in the browser*

As you've seen, it's very easy to create, publish, and view Visio drawings on SharePoint platform. Now let's discuss some of the features and capabilities of Visio Services.

Visio Services Features

- Visio diagrams are compatible with Internet Explorer, Mozilla Firefox, and Apple Safari.

- In SharePoint 2013, diagrams are no longer rendered using Silverlight but are rendered as high-quality PNG(s) for full fidelity.

    - You can connect data to shapes in a diagram from various supported data sources (see Chapter 3).

    - You can use a variety of data graphics for a given data field, and corresponding shapes based on the conditions and data. Figure 2-11 shows the idea at a very high level (see Chapter 3).

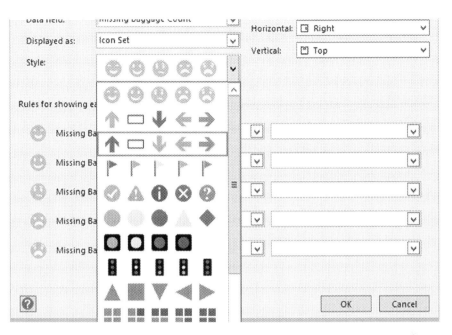

Figure 2-11. *Data graphics that can be used on shapes*

- You can set hyperlinks on the shapes. You can link to an Internet address or another local Visio diagram, as shown in Figures 2-12 and 2-13.

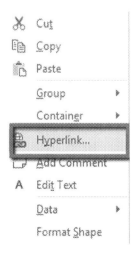

Figure 2-12. *Adding a hyperlink to a shape*

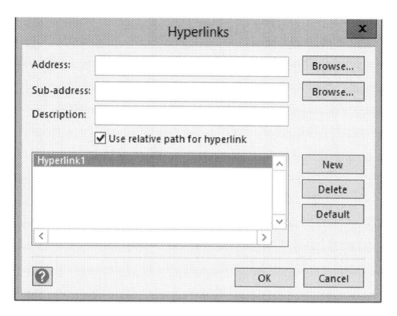

Figure 2-13. *Linking a shape to an Internet address or local file*

- No client-side installation is required—diagrams are fully loaded in the client browser.

- Real-time data refresh means you can connect your diagrams with real-time data using various data sources, including:

  - SQL Server

  - Excel workbook

  - SharePoint Foundation Lists

  - OLE DB

  - ODBC

  - Custom data providers

  - Business Connectivity Services (BCS)

■ **Caution**   Some data sources, such as SQL Server Analysis Services, are not supported.

- Publish once, use multiple times. You can create the diagrams, connect them to data, and publish them to your SharePoint environment. The diagrams load data from the underlying data sources and you won't have to modify them unless and until the source diagrams change. When the data changes, the shapes will automatically reflect the changes.

- Various authentication models (explained further in chapter 4) are supported, including

  - Secure Store Services (SSS) (explained further in chapter 4)

  - Kerberos or Integrated Windows Authentication

  - Unattended Authentication

▓ **Info**   In Chapter 4, we will discuss how to connect to a SQL Server data source, a SharePoint Server list, and a custom data provider, with examples.

In our first example, you saw how to publish a Visio drawing to SharePoint and view it. That's one of the ways to integrate Visio with SharePoint. There are a number of other methods for loading and interacting with a Visio drawing on SharePoint 2013, including:

- Visio Web Access Web Part—Use a Web part that can load a .vsdx file.

- JavaScript Mashup API—Communicate with a Visio Web Access Web part and change HTML content as needed asynchronously.

- Web Part connections—Connect and communicate with other Web parts on the page.

- SharePoint Designer with Visio—Create diagrams in Visio, import them into SharePoint Designer, and publish them to the SharePoint environment.

- Commenting: Users can share their views and collaborate with others using the new commenting feature.

We'll discuss these in Chapter 4, but first we'll take a look the architecture and building blocks of Visio Services.

Architecture

Figure 2-14 shows the components a Visio Services environment. Visio Services is loaded into and becomes an integral part of SharePoint Server 2013, which runs on Windows Server 2012 in conjunction with IIS, SQL Server, and Windows Identity foundation. Visio Services can run in both hosted and nonhosted environments.

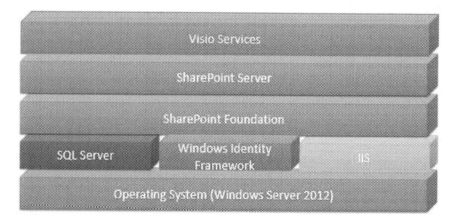

Figure 2-14. *The architecture of a Visio Services 2013 environment*

■ **Note** Hosted environments are platforms provided by external vendors on which you can run your own applications. You may have some access to the physical servers and file system, but it can be rather limited. Still, this can be a very cost-effective solution and may reduce a lot of your operating costs. Nonhosted or in-house environments, by contrast, are fully controlled by your own organization. These are physical servers commissioned in your own network to which you have full access.

To understand the architecture, let's take a look at the life cycle of a Visio drawing, as shown in Figure 2-15. A designer or a business analyst retrieves data from one of the supported data sources and creates a Visio diagram. He or she saves the file as a drawing file (.vsdx), then uploads or publishes the diagram into the SharePoint Server document library. Visio Services then renders this document by accessing the data source and displaying the output to the end user(s) as a PNG file. Note that you don't actually need a data source.

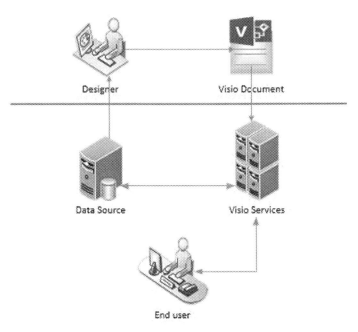

Figure 2-15. *Life cycle of a Visio diagram*

Now here's the interesting part: the designer who creates the diagram may not be a part of the entire life cycle of the diagram. He doesn't need to have any knowledge of SharePoint. He can simply create the designs and provide them to the next level in the hierarchy who can publish them to SharePoint. End users will access the diagrams through application servers and view them in the browser directly. However, the process of publishing a diagram to Visio Services is simple.

Summary

In this chapter, you have learnt about configuring Visio services, published a basic Visio diagram to SharePoint, and gained an understanding of the architecture and features of Visio Services.

What's Next?

In the next chapter, you will learn more about Visio 2013 features relevant to Visio Services, with the use of the Visio client Data tab.

CHAPTER 3

Visio Data Tab

In this chapter, we'll see how Visio lets you bind your web drawings to real data.

To bind data to a data source in the Visio 2013 client, you use the options accessed by clicking on the Data tab of the ribbon (Figure 3-1). To enable all of the buttons that belong to this tab, you should have at least one diagram open.

Figure 3-1. *Data tab in Visio 2013*

Let's understand what each button does in turn.

Link Data to Shapes

Link Data to Shapes is one of the ways you can connect a data source to a shape. You get a simple Data Selector wizard that connects to various supported data sources, as shown in Figure 3-2. You can create more than one data source using this option and use them to connect data to the shapes.

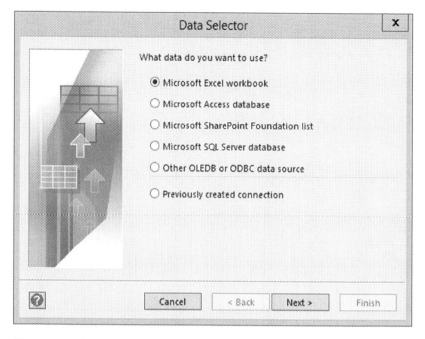

Figure 3-2. *The Data Selector window*

░ **Note** Another way to create a data source is by using VBA code, as you'll see when we look at designing a custom data provider.

Data Graphics

Data Graphics is the mechanism that lets you connect data to the shape and customize the appearance of the shape. It allows you to add visual information about the data to the shape on the Visio diagram. You can build your own data graphic, assign it to any data field, and display the corresponding value in one of these forms: Text, Data Bar, Icon Set, or Color by Value. Data fields are the columns that belong to a list or data table available through the data source you selected.

Data Graphics define additional design structures for the shape, and you can create more than one. Once you set your own custom data graphics, they can be used on any other shapes on the Visio diagram using the Automatically Link button.

Data Graphics get data from the data source specified in Link Data to Shapes or Shape Data Window (explained in the "Shape Data Window" section). When you link to the data source, the data graphics display real-time or historical information based on the customizations that you've set on the Visio Graphics Services in the Central Administration.

Here's how to create new Data Graphics:

1. Click on the Data Graphics icon on the Data tab. This displays a settings window, as shown in Figure 3-3.

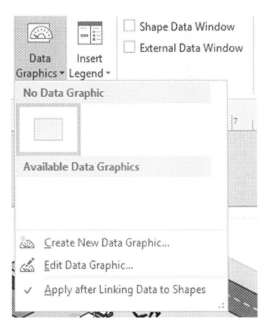

Figure 3-3. *Creating a new Data Graphic*

2. Click Create New Data Graphic... to open a New Data Graphic window.

3. Click New Item, and a new window opens that with settings for display and position, as shown in Figure 3-4.

21

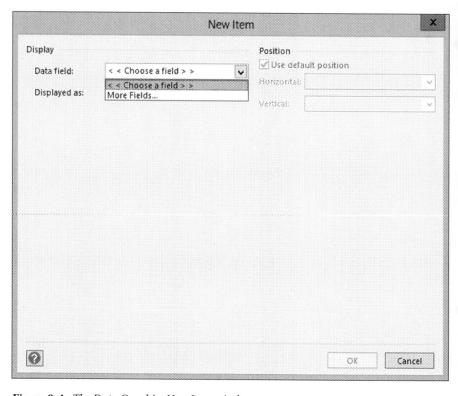

Figure 3-4. *The Data Graphics New Item window*

4. In the display section, the Data field drop-down consists of the available fields from the connected data source. When there's no data source, few fields are displayed. If you need a data field and don't have a data source, you can define a custom shape data label that can be used as a data field in this context.

5. To create a custom shape data label, right-click on the shape on your diagram and, from the Data menu, select Define Shape Data... In the window that opens, enter the Label as "Text" (or your own custom label); select the Type as String (or whatever data type you need); set the Value to a specific data value, and optionally configure other settings if necessary, and click OK.

6. The label will now appear in the Data field drop-down in the data graphics New Item window.

7. Once you select your new Data field label, the 'Displayed as' drop-down is enabled and has options for Text, Data Bar, Icon Set, and Color by Value. For this example, let's go with the Text option. Choosing Text in the 'Displayed as' field displays the Style drop-down, with various options.

8. Once you've chosen the style, you can use the Position section to set the style either horizontally or vertically for the shape. For instance, if you want to display the value of the Text within a Circle callout and position it horizontally to the Right and vertically at the Bottom of the shape, the settings would be similar to those in Figure 3-5.

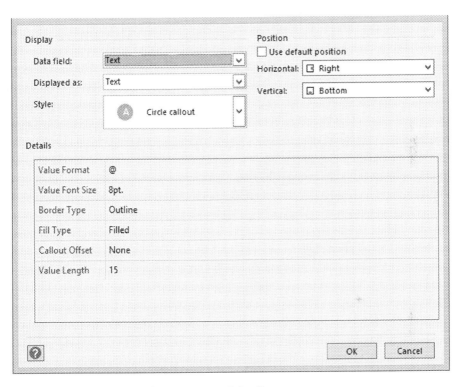

Figure 3-5. *Set data field styles, position, and details*

9. In the Details section, you can set the data field metadata values. For instance, @ in the Value Format field represents Text format.

10. Click OK to return to the New Data Graphic window.

11. You can edit an existing item by clicking Edit Item, and you can delete an item by clicking the Delete button. Click OK to close the wizard.

12. You can also set the value of the shape using the Shape Data Window that's available when you check this option in the Show/Hide section of the Data tab. You can set the Text value and view how the value is displayed for the shape. For instance, to set the Text value for the flight shape as "Passenger Airplane," select the shape and on the Shape Data Window, type in Passenger Airplane. The text will appear in the bottom right corner of the image as a call out, as per the previous position settings (Figure 3-6).

Figure 3-6. *Adding text to the shape*

▓ **Note** You can obtain this shape from More Shapes ➤ Visio Extras ➤ Symbols (US units) ➤ Airport.

▓ **Tip** You'll notice the same text label beneath the shape; this is the general text that comes with the shape and it's what would be used as a condition for automatically linking other shapes.

Automatically Link

To use the Data tab's Automatically Link functionality, first you need to set a Text value either by double-clicking on the shape or by using the Shape Data Window on all the shapes. Using the Data Graphics option, you can create items based on data fields (as shown in the previous section). First, you will have to create a complete data graphic for at least one shape. After you create the data sources, you can bind a shape to a row of data by simply dragging and dropping the row onto the shape. This process creates a link between the shape text, the data column name (for instance Title), and the column values of the row. This is the final step before linking all the shapes. Click on the Automatically Link button in the External Data section of the Data tab. The wizard lets you decide whether to link 'Selected shapes' or 'All shapes on this page', as shown in Figure 3-7.

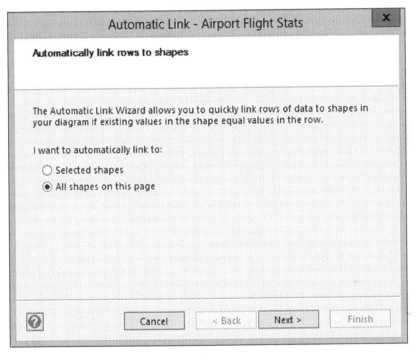

Figure 3-7. Automatically link data to shapes

Choosing one of these options takes you to the next step—mapping the Data Column to the Shape Field, as shown in Figure 3-8. Click Next to reach the Details page, or click Finish to complete the automatic linking. This step links all shapes with the text matching the Data Column name.

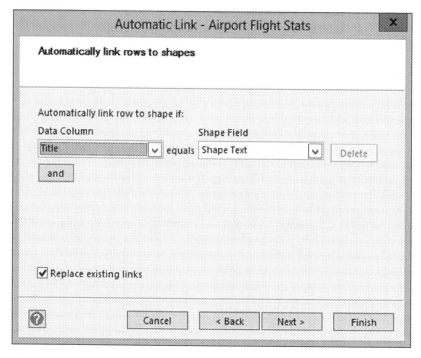

Figure 3-8. *Link a data column to a shape field*

Refresh All

Once you have created the data sources using Link Data to Shapes, you can refresh them either individually or all at once to get the updated data. When you hover on the Refresh All button, it opens a context menu, as shown in Figure 3-9.

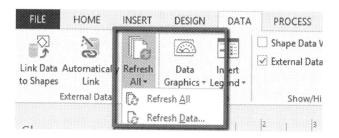

Figure 3-9. *Refresh All data window*

Note   Using Refresh All or Refresh Data doesn't affect SharePoint in any way. These options work only with respect to the Visio diagram and the related data source.

You can choose the data source (if one is available) and click on either Refresh or Refresh All to refresh the available data sources, as shown in Figure 3-10. Either action will connect to the data source and retrieve the most recent data. Choosing the data source and clicking on Configure... opens the data source configuration wizard. If no data source was configured earlier, none would be listed in this window.

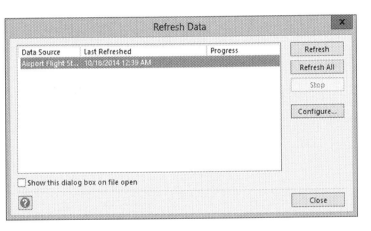

Figure 3-10. *Refresh Data window*

Insert Legend

Use Insert Legend to display information regarding Data Bar, Icon Set, or Color by Value display options available from the Data Graphics dialog. Legends display information related to the existing page. You can set the legend direction to be either horizontal or vertical. However, legends are not automatically updated. If you modify the diagram, legends need to be manually deleted and inserted once again to reflect the changes.

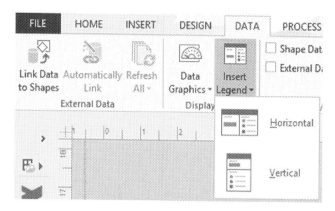

Figure 3-11. Insert Legend wizard

Shape Data Window

The Shape Data Window is available by checking the appropriate box on the Data tab. It displays data information about the shape, and you can also set the data values for the shape, as shown in Figure 3-12.

Wood Fence Thickness	5
Wood Post Type	Round
Wood Post Size	5.5 in.
Masonry Fence Thickness	10 in.
Masonry Post Type	Round
Masonry Post Size	18 in.
Stone Fence Thickness	12 in.
Chain Link Fence Thickness	3 in.
Metal Post Type	Round
Metal Post Size	3 in.
Road Thickness	0.0625 in.

Figure 3-12. Shape Data window

External Data Window

You can check the External Data Window box on the Data tab to make this window accessible. It displays all of the available data sources for a given page of the Visio diagram, and you can create a new data source by clicking on Link Data to Shapes... as shown in Figure 3-13.

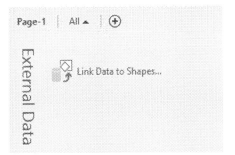

Figure 3-13. *External data window*

   With the help of these options and settings, you can design the Visio diagrams with shapes, connect the shapes to data, and then publish the drawings to a SharePoint environment. In the next chapter, you'll see how to integrate all that you've learned so far with Visio and Visio Services.

Summary

In this chapter, you have learned about Visio 2013 features relevant to Visio Services and various tabs and their uses.

What's Next?

In the next chapter, you will learn about integrating Visio diagrams with SharePoint, configuration, and connecting to various data sources.

CHAPTER 4

Integrating Visio with SharePoint

So far, you have seen how to integrate Visio diagrams with SharePoint at a very high level. Now you'll learn this practically, using some examples.

Let's create a Visio diagram using a SharePoint list as a data source and see how to deploy the diagram to the SharePoint platform.

Creating Data-Powered Visio Diagrams

In this example, we can see how to populate a Visio diagram with real data from a SharePoint list, and publish this data-powered diagram to SharePoint.

PROBLEM CASE

Take the Airport flight status example and populate information from a SharePoint list to the diagram, then publish the diagram to the SharePoint environment and view it with real-time data.

Solution

Open SharePoint site and create a custom list with the name Airport Flight Stats, with columns as shown in Figure 4-1.

Columns

A column stores information about each item in the list. The following columns

Column (click to edit)	Type	Required
Title	Single line of text	✓
Number of flights run	Number	
Number of flights cancelled	Number	
On Time Arrivals	Number	
On Time Departures	Number	
Delayed Arrivals	Number	
Delayed Departures	Number	
Missing Baggage Count	Number	
Number of missing flights	Number	
Crew Strikes Count	Number	
Modified	Date and Time	
Created	Date and Time	
Created By	Person or Group	
Modified By	Person or Group	

Figure 4-1. *Sample custom SharePoint list structure*

Populate a few rows of data for various airline carriers, as in Figure 4-2.

Figure 4-2. *Custom list with data used as a data source*

When you've created the list, open Visio.

Open the Airport.vsd file and click on the Link Data to Shapes icon either on the Data tab or from the External Data pane at the bottom of the page (Figure 4-3).

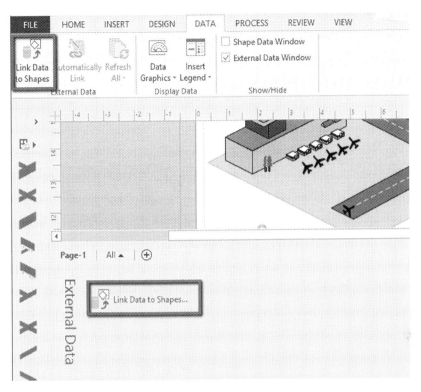

Figure 4-3. *Accessing Link Data to Shapes to build a data source*

From the Data Selector window, choose the Microsoft SharePoint Foundation list option and click Next.

Enter the URL for the site where you created the custom list and click Next.

On the Data Selector window, choose Airport Flight Stats from the List box and select the option Link to a list. You can also create a View on the custom list and choose Link to a view of a list. Click Next to continue.

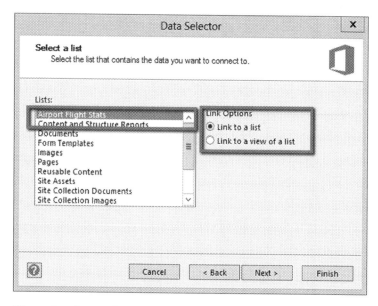

Figure 4-4. *Data Selector Window*

On the final screen, click Finish to complete the Data Selector wizard.

If External Data Window is checked on the Data tab, you should now have the External Data window visible at the bottom of the screen with the custom list data loaded, as shown in Figure 4-5. Notice that the list name is added to the External Data Source window at the bottom.

ID	Title	Number of flights run	Number of flights cancelled	On Time Arrivals	On Time Dep
1	British Airways	365	12	300	315
2	Air France	300	15	270	280
3	US Airways	250	0	245	248
4	Lufthansa	290	1	285	282
5	Malaysian Airlines	275	4	261	270

Airport Flight Stats

Figure 4-5. *External Data window populated with selected data*

To link data to the shape, simply drag one of the rows to a particular shape on the page. If the data is properly linked, you'll see a link icon in the External Data window next to the row (first column), as shown in Figure 4-6. Alternatively, you can select the shape first and right-click on the row you'd like to bind. Then, from the context menu, choose the option Link to Selected Shapes.

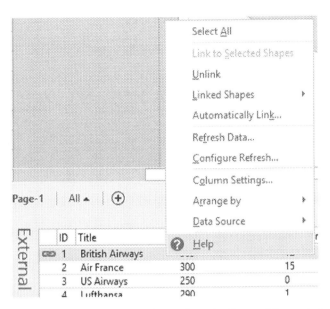

Figure 4-6. Linking data to shapes from the External Data window

As you can see, you can also disconnect the row data from the shape using the Unlink option from the context menu.

When all the rows are linked, the leftmost columns will display link icons for all the rows (Figure 4-7).

	Title	Number of flights run
	British Airways	365
	Air France	300
	US Airways	250
	Lufthansa	290
	Malaysian Airlines	275

Airport Flight Stats

Figure 4-7. Icons showing that all rows are linked

■ **Caution**   If there is any mismatch between the column name and the text on the shapes, the linking will not work. Also, if you add a new row of data, you'll need to create a new shape and link the row data to that shape.

Click on Data Graphics and choose the 'Create New Data Graphic' option.

Click on New Item and from the Data field choose 'Delayed Arrivals', and from the 'Displayed as' options, choose 'Icon Set'.

From Style, choose the face icons as shown in Figure 4-8.

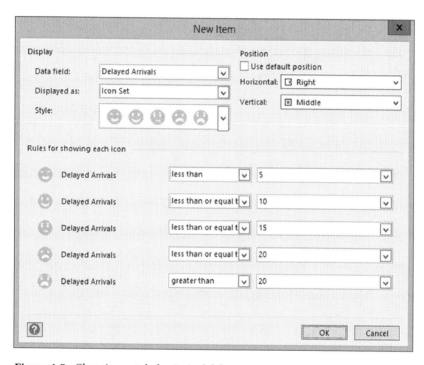

Figure 4-8. *Choosing a style for Arrival delays*

Under the Rules for showing each icon, set the conditions and values for each icon as shown in Figure 4-8.

Choose the position as Right for Horizontal and Top for Vertical and click OK.

Once again from the New Data Graphic window, click on 'New Item' and, in the Data field, choose 'Missing Baggage Count'.

Under the 'Displayed as' option, choose 'Data Bar' and select 'Star rating' as the Style.

In the Details section, set Minimum Value to 18 and Maximum Value to 0 and leave the other options as is, as shown in Figure 4-9. Uncheck 'Use default position' and set Horizontal to Center and Vertical to Top and click OK.

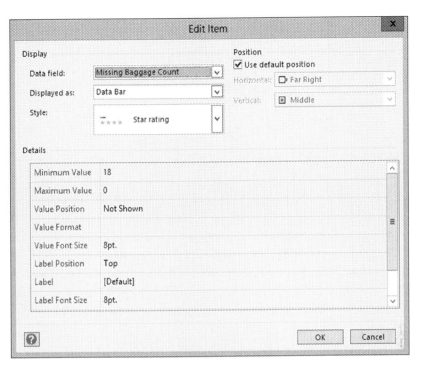

Figure 4-9. *Choosing a style for Missing baggage count*

▒ **Note**   Because the maximum baggage count by any airline carrier in this example is 18, we'll use this for easy comparison.

Return to the New Data Graphic window and notice the two data field settings. If you click either Apply or OK, an alert asks "Do you want to apply this data graphic to the selected shapes?" Click Yes to close the prompt.

Notice the two icon sets that are displayed for the British Airways flight; with the available data (Figure 4-10), the graphic must display ratings in the center top position and a frown icon in the right top corner.

Figure 4-10. *Data graphics set to the shape*

Select other shapes and link corresponding rows of information to them as described earlier.

▓ **Tip** Alternatively, select each of the shapes in the diagram and set the Text property for each. Each Text value should have the same text as in the Title of the data source. For instance, if you want to set the first shape to British Airways, you have to make sure the text exactly matches the text in the Title column of the data source.

Use the Automatically Link button on the Data tab, and choose the 'All Shapes on this page' option, then click Next. From the 'Automatically link rows to shapes' window, choose Title from the Data Column, and from the Shape Field select Shape Text. Leave the default option of 'Replace existing links' and click Next. View the final summary window and click the Finish button. Data source rows are now automatically linked to shapes.

After performing these steps, you'll see that star ratings and frown icon styles are set for all the other shapes according to the data, as shown in Figure 4-11.

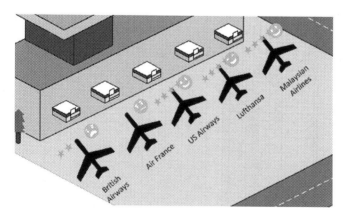

Figure 4-11. *Completed Visio diagram with data graphics set*

Now that your Visio diagram is ready, go ahead and publish it to your SharePoint environment.

From the File menu, select Save As and choose the 'Save to SharePoint' option, select the Web Drawing File Type, and click the Save As button. Choose the previously saved location, and save the file as Airport.vsdx, overwriting the existing file.

You can now save the drawing file to the SharePoint Online site as well. From Backstage view, click on Save As and choose 'Add a Place' and select Office 365 SharePoint, as shown in Figure 4-12.

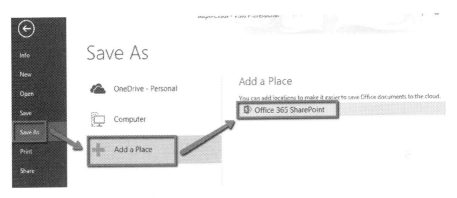

Figure 4-12. *Visio 2013 Save As options*

In the 'Add a service' window, type the email address you used while registering with Office 365 subscription or the account provisioned for you, as shown in Figure 4-13.

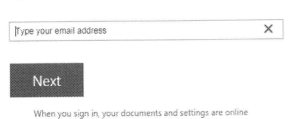

Figure 4-13. *Office 365 SharePoint Online Add a service*

If the email is recognized by Office 365, you will be challenged with a login screen, as shown in Figure 4-14. Enter your User ID, Password and click 'Sign in'.

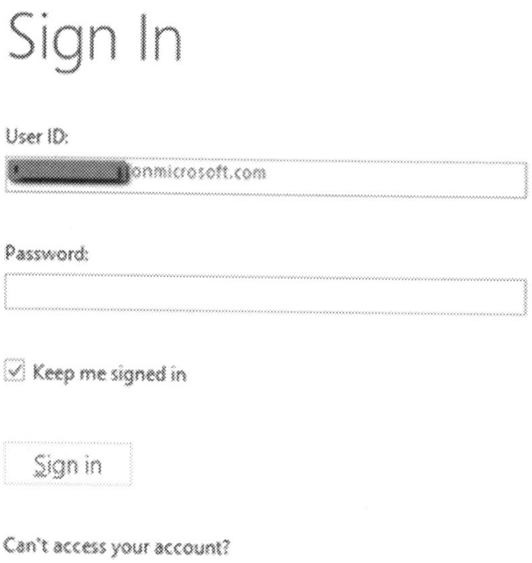

Sign In

User ID:

[████████onmicrosoft.com]

Password:

[   ]

☑ Keep me signed in

[Sign in]

Can't access your account?

Figure 4-14. *SharePoint Online Sign In screen*

Once authenticated, you will have the option to choose between SharePoint Online sites that are available for you along with OneDrive option. Choose the site you wish to save your .vsdx file and click on 'Browse' button, as shown in Figure 4-15.

Save As

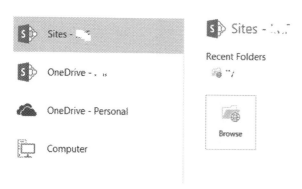

Figure 4-15. *SharePoint Online Save As options*

You will then be prompted with window where you can choose the document library to save the Visio document, as shown in Figure 4-16.

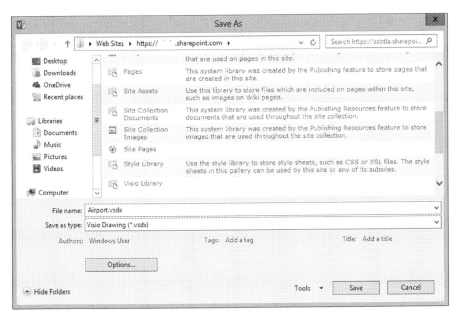

Figure 4-16. *SharePoint Online Document Library Save As option*

▓ **Tip**   You can decide to not overwrite the file it by choosing another file name, such as Airport_with_data.vdw.

Access your SharePoint site and open the Visio Library document library.

Click on Add document, then browse and choose the .vsdx file and click OK.

Click on the .vsdx document and notice that the Visio diagram opens in a full browser window with the diagram and shapes connected to the SharePoint list data, as shown in Figure 4-17.

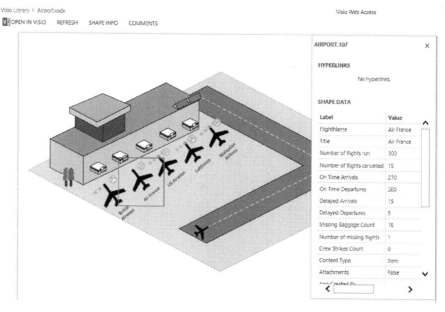

Figure 4-17. *Visio drawing*

Return to the Airport Flight Stats custom list and edit the Lufthansa item. Change the 'Delayed Arrivals' column value to 14 and 'Missing baggage count' value to 15 and click on Save.

Return to the Visio Library document library and click on the airport.vsdx drawing file. Notice that the Lufthansa flight data graphic styles have changed based on the new values.

▓ **Note**   In order to get real-time values, you'll want to set the Minimum and Maximum Cache Age Value to zero. You'll find these under Global Settings for Visio Graphics Service on the Central Administration screen (explained later in this chapter).

Note that if an error occurs during the loading of Visio drawing, a static image of the drawing will be displayed instead of error messages.

You've already seen how to view Visio diagrams in the SharePoint environment by clicking on the .vsdx file in the document library; this opens the diagram in full-screen mode in the browser. Well, this may not be what you want in every situation. You might want to display diagrams on a page with other web parts or you may be connecting to information with other web parts. For such cases, you can use the Visio Web Access web part.

Using the Visio Web Access Web Part

To have this functionality, be sure to activate the SharePoint Server Enterprise Site Collection Feature. You can access the Visio Web Access (VWA) web part, which is available out of the box, under the Business Data Category. To add this web part, click on Edit Page icon. Click on page content and from the insert tab select Web Part. Under the categories, choose Business Data and select 'Visio Web Access' web part, as shown in Figure 4-18. Click on the 'Add' button to insert the web part to the page.

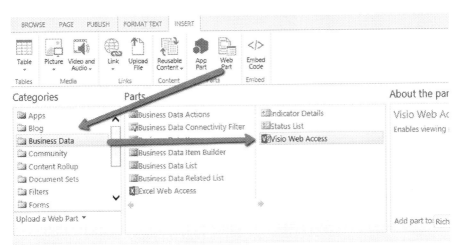

Figure 4-18. *Choosing Visio Web Access web part*

The VWA web part seeks the .vsdx file path to display the drawings. Use the "Click here to open the tool pane" link and choose the .vsdx file from your Visio Library, as shown in Figure 4-19, then click OK.

Select an Asset

Current Location: Visio Library at http://sp/Visio Library

Figure 4-19. *Choosing a Visio drawing file for the Visio Web Access web part*

On the tool pane, leave all the defaults as is and click the OK button at the bottom. The .vsdx file is now loaded and you can view the diagram with data, as shown in Figure 4-20.

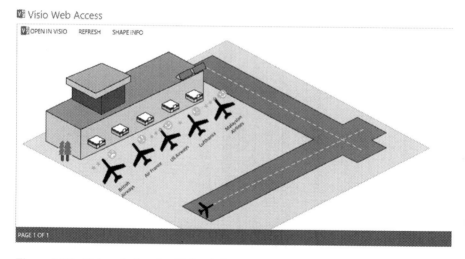

Figure 4-20. *Visio web drawing file loaded using Visio Web Access web part*

The Visio Web Access web part header includes a number of options:

- Open in Visio: opens the file in either Read-Only or Edit mode, assuming you have the Visio client installed on your machine.

- Refresh: refreshes the data on the current page of the diagram. You can have more than one page in a diagram.

- Choose Page: displays any page from the web drawing.

- Zoom in/out: zooms the image from 10 to 200 percent.

- Zoom to fit page to view: fits the diagram to the web part height and width.

- Shape Info: displays a Shape Information pane (movable on the diagram) that provides Shape Data and any hyperlinks on the shape.

Note You can move the image in any direction by clicking and holding the left mouse button. You can use the scroll button on your mouse to zoom the diagram in or out.

Visio Web Access Web Part Connections

Visio Web Access web parts support two-way communications, providing rich interaction with other web parts on the page. They can act as both consumer and provider. Web part connections can be directly configured in the browser.

Tip After configuring the connections, if you use the view source option of the browser to view the page, you'll notice that these web part connections are built using JavaScript.

There are many scenarios in which these connections can be helpful. You have already seen how to use a VWA web part that can load a .vsdx file and connect to a SharePoint list. Let's use the same SharePoint list and try to filter the information and reveal the shape that results from the filter criteria:

1. Create a new site page (Airport Stats.aspx in this case) and add the VWA web part. Configure it to load the airport_with_data.vsdx drawing file or the Airport.vdw file if you haven't saved the file with a different name. Also add the list web part (Airport Flight Stats), as shown in Figure 4-21.

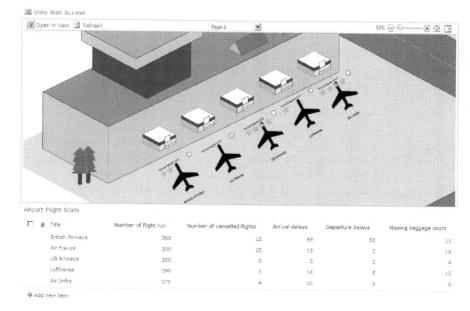

Figure 4-21. Adding the drawing file (using a VWA web part) and custom list to the page

2. From the VWA web part menu, click on 'Edit Web Part' link. Once again from the VWA web part menu, choose Connections ➤ Get Filter Results From ➤ Airport Flight Stats, as shown in Figure 4-22.

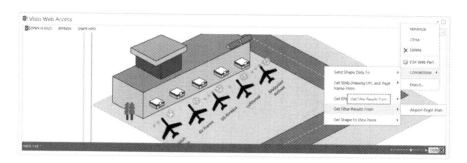

Figure 4-22. Visio Web Access web part connections

3. Click on Apply or OK on the editor pane.

4. Now apply the filter on the Airport Flight Stats list for the Number of cancelled flights column and choose 15.

5. As soon as the filter is applied, notice that the shape with corresponding value is selected, as shown in Figure 4-23.

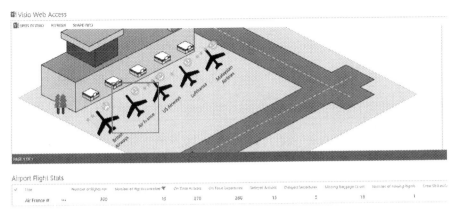

Figure 4-23. *Visio Web Access web part connections with filtered data*

▓ **Tip** You can use web part connections with any list to obtain filtered data results on the drawing, assuming there is information to filter. If there's no filtered information, you will not see any results.

Here are the various connection options:

- Send Shape Data To (provider): sends shape data to any other web part on the page.

- Get Web Drawing URL and Page Name From (consumer): gets diagram URL from another web part on the page to render.

- Get Shapes to Highlight From (consumer): gets shape name from another web part to highlight the corresponding shape.

- Get Filter Results From (consumer): gets shape data values from another web part to highlight the shapes based on the values provided.

- Get Shape to View: gets and zooms to the shape provided.

▓ **Note** If you need to configure advanced options, you might have to use SharePoint Designer. You can extend and build custom interfaces to address connections to other web parts on the page using the IWebPartParameters interface. For more details, visit `http://msdn.microsoft.com/en-us/library/system.web.ui.webcontrols.webparts.iwebpartparameters(v=vs.110).aspx`.

So far, you've seen publishing Visio drawings either with data (using a SharePoint list) or without data. Now let's see how to connect using SQL Server as a data source, publish the diagrams to SharePoint, and configure security options.

Using a SQL Server Data Source

Now that you've seen how to establish a data connection with a SharePoint list, let's try to connect a Visio diagram to a SQL Server table. First, of course, you'll need to create a database table and then populate the table with some data.

PROBLEM CASE

Display Washington, D.C., mall monuments with the number of visitors in a year and the landmarks' popularity ratings. Publish this diagram to SharePoint and use Visio Services to display real-time data.

Solution

Create a new database named VisioServices.

Create a table named "tblLandmarks" in the new database and create the columns shown in Figure 4-24. Populate the columns with data, as shown in Figure 4-25.

```
⊟ ◯ VisioServices
   ⊞ 🗀 Database Diagrams
   ⊟ 🗀 Tables
      ⊞ 🗀 System Tables
      ⊟ ▦ dbo.tblLandmarks
         ⊟ 🗀 Columns
               🔑 LandmarkID (PK, int, not null)
               ▦ Landmark (nvarchar(50), not null)
               ▦ YearBuilt (int, not null)
               ▦ Details (nvarchar(100), null)
               ▦ Ratings (decimal(18,0), not null)
               ▦ Visitors (bigint, null)
         ⊞ 🗀 Keys
         ⊞ 🗀 Constraints
         ⊞ 🗀 Triggers
         ⊞ 🗀 Indexes
         ⊞ 🗀 Statistics
```

Figure 4-24. *Design a custom SQL table structure*

	LandmarkID	Landmark	YearBuilt	Details	Ratings	Visitors
1	1	White House	1792	The White House is the official residence and princip...	5	614000
2	2	Federal Triangle	1900	The Federal Triangle is an area just North of the Nati...	5	412000
3	3	Museum of American History	1964	The National Museum of American History is an ever ...	5	525765
4	4	Gallery of Art	1937	The National Gallery of Art houses a permanent colle...	4	435000
5	5	US Capitol	1793	The US Capitol is the meeting place of the United St. .	5	415732
6	6	Washington Monument	1840	The Wahington Monument is one of the many famou...	4	785455
7	7	Museum of Natural History	1910	National Museum of Natural History houses the major...	4	121548
8	8	Freer Gallery of Art	1923	The Freer Gallery of Art contains art from East Asia, S...	4	154547
9	9	Hirshhorn Museum	1974	The Hishhorn Museum contains over 10.000 paintings	4	245623
10	10	Air and Space Museum	1976	Washington's National Air and Space Museum attrac...	5	554564
11	11	Museum of the American Indian	2004	An exciting new museum that tells the story of the US...	4	440546
12	12	Arts and Industries	1879	The Arts and Industries building is the second oldest ...	3	457524

Figure 4-25. *Populating the custom table with sample data*

Open Visio 2013 and create a new diagram. From More Shapes ➤ Maps and Floor Plans ➤ Map, choose Landmark Shapes (US Units) and add some of the available shapes to the page. Provide Titles for all the shapes either by using the Shape Data window or the shape's label. When you create each label, make sure it matches the values in the Landmark column in Figure 4-25.

Use Link Data to Shapes and choose the Microsoft SQL Server database option, then click Next.

In the Data Connection wizard, enter the Server name and the Log-on credentials, either Windows Authentication or User Name and Password. Click Next to continue.

▦ **Note**   While communicating with SQL Server through Visio Services, you'll need to configure an additional setting. If you're using SQL Server with Windows Authentication, you'd connect using:

Kerberos/Integrated Windows Authentication: This setting uses the current logged-in user account, which requires Kerberos delegation to authenticate to the database server. For more information on Kerberos, see
`http://technet.microsoft.com/en-us/magazine/ee914605.aspx`.

Secure Store Service (SSS): This setting uses either an individual user or group that's mapped for authentication while using an office data connection file (*.ODC). SSS is explained in more detail later in this chapter.

Unattended Service Account: This is a low-privilege Windows account mapped to a target application that is impersonated while connecting to the database. (This is also what you'd use with SQL Authentication.) We will be using this model with SSS while connecting to SQL Server as a data source.

From the available databases, choose VisioServices and select the tblLandmarks table. Click Next to continue.

The next step gives you the option to save the data connection file (.odc) as a physical file. Click on Browse to choose where to save the .odc file (or skip this step by clicking on Finish). The .odc file can be repurposed to create a new data source connection from the Data Selector window by choosing the previously created connection option. Provide a friendly name for the file and click Finish to complete the wizard.

▦ **Note**   To create a data-refreshable web drawing (.vsdx), you have to save the .odc file to the same SharePoint site location as the data connection library.

Under the 'Data Selector' screen, choose the columns and rows to include and click Next to continue. After a successful import message, click Finish.

The External Data window will now load and display the data from the selected database table.

Make sure that the text in the Landmark column is identical to the Title of the shapes. Drag row data from the External Data window to the shape on the page. If the column text is identical to the shape text, the link will be created successfully and you can then create the data graphics for the shape.

Create the Data Graphics as explained earlier and choose the Ratings data field. Uncheck Use default position and set the custom position for the Data Bar Style as horizontally Center and vertically Above Shape.

Add the Visitors data field and choose the Thermometer Data Bar Style. Position it Far Right horizontally and Middle vertically. Click OK to close the data graphics wizard.

Use the Automatically Link all shapes option to connect all the rows of data to the respective shapes. Choose the data column Landmark to match the shape field Shape Text and click on the Finish button.

Now use the Insert Legend option to name the page "DC Landmarks."

The web drawing should now look like the one in Figure 4-26.

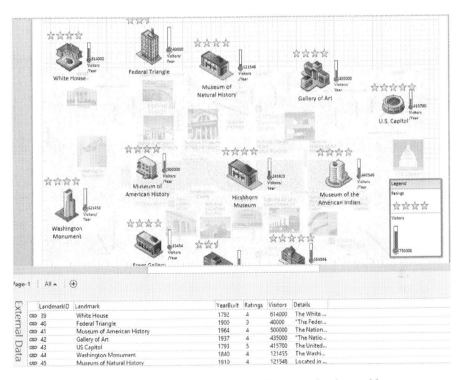

Figure 4-26. *Visio drawing shapes connected to a SQL Server database table*

■ **Tip** I created the diagram in Figure 4-26 on a blank stencil using images and shapes from Landmark Shapes (US units).

If the data changes and you want to make sure the drawing reflects the updates, choose either of Refresh All or Refresh Data on the Data tab.

Choosing either of these opens the Refresh Data window (Figure 4-27), which displays all data sources related to this diagram. You can refresh one data source or all of them together. To configure a data source, just select it and choose Configure. Close the window when you're finished.

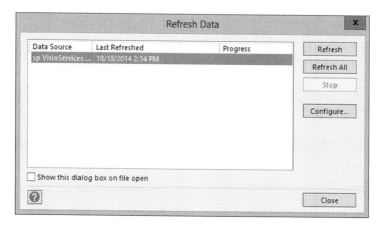

Figure 4-27. *The Refresh Data window*

Now that you finished the diagram, go ahead and publish it to the SharePoint environment. Choose File ➤ Save & Send ➤ Save to SharePoint ➤ Web Drawing ➤ Save As to save the file physically to your disk as Mall.vsdx.

Open the SharePoint site and upload Mall.vsdx to the Visio Library.

Click on the Visio drawing you uploaded and view the drawing that is rendered in the browser. If the drawing is loading for the first time, you will be prompted about disabled refresh option. You can choose to 'Allow Refresh' by clicking on the appropriate button as shown in Figure 4-28.

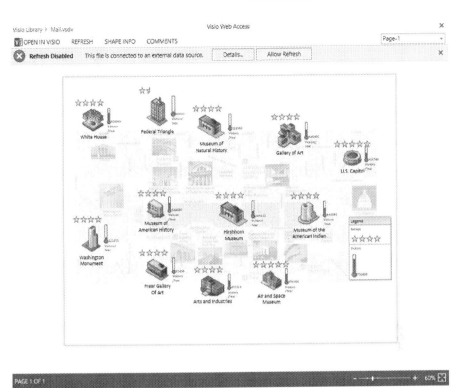

Figure 4-28. *Visio diagram refresh disabled warning*

If SQL Server is on the same machine, the drawing will render correctly. However, if you are accessing SQL Server from a different machine or if you are on a domain controller, you'll see the error shown in Figure 4-29.

Figure 4-29. *Error refreshing the data connection in the Web drawing*

This error is caused by a scenario known as the **double-hop issue**.

The Double-Hop Issue

Take a look at the error message in Figure 4-29. Basically, this means that although you can use impersonated credentials locally, Windows won't forward impersonated credentials to a remote resource (the second hop), so the user's identity is lost even before reaching the back end. And in this scenario SharePoint can't pass the credentials of the logged-in user all the way to the back end via the services.

What you need is a mechanism by which the logged-in user is impersonated "as someone else" to use Visio services and connect to the back end data. You can achieve this by using the Secure Store Services (SSS) in SharePoint.

Secure Store Services

You can consider Secure Store Services the next generation of the single sign-on service that is introduced in SharePoint 2010. SSS is a credential store that saves account information securely in the database.

You can create and set these credentials on a per application basis associated to an Application Id and use this Application Id for different services that are subject to the double-hop issue. You can consider SSS as a gatekeeper service for authenticating a user (or a group) against an application. You can also set ID for each target application at the farm level.

Configuring Secure Store Services

1. Make sure that you are a Farm Administrator and log on to the Central Administration site.

2. Click on Application Management and choose Manage Service Applications from the Service Applications group (Figure 4-30).

Application Management

Web Applications
Manage web applications
Configure alternate access mappings

Site Collections
Create site collections | Delete a site collection
Confirm site use and deletion | Specify quota templates
Configure quotas and locks
Change site collection administrators
View all site collections | Configure self-service site creation

Service Applications
Manage service applications
Configure service application associations

Databases
Manage content databases
Specify the default database server
Configure the data retrieval service

Figure 4-30. *Choose Manage service applications on the Central Administration site*

3. From the list of available services, click on the Secure Store
Service (Figure 4-31).

PowerPoint Conversion Service Application	PowerPoint Conversion :
Search Administration Web Service for Search Service Application	Search Administration W
Search Service Application	Search Service Applicatic
Search Service Application	Search Service Applicatic
Secure Store Service	Secure Store Service App
Secure Store Service	Secure Store Service App
Security Token Service Application	Security Token Service A
SettingsServiceApp	Microsoft SharePoint Fo Application
Microsoft SharePoint Foundation Subscription Settings Service Application Proxy	Microsoft SharePoint Fo Application Proxy

Figure 4-31. *Choose Secure Store Service*

On the Secure Store Service page, set the following options:

- Generate New Key: Before beginning to create a new target
application, you need to generate a new key from a pass phrase
(Figure 4-32). This key is used to encrypt and decrypt credentials
that are stored in the database. You must have Administrator
rights to create a key.

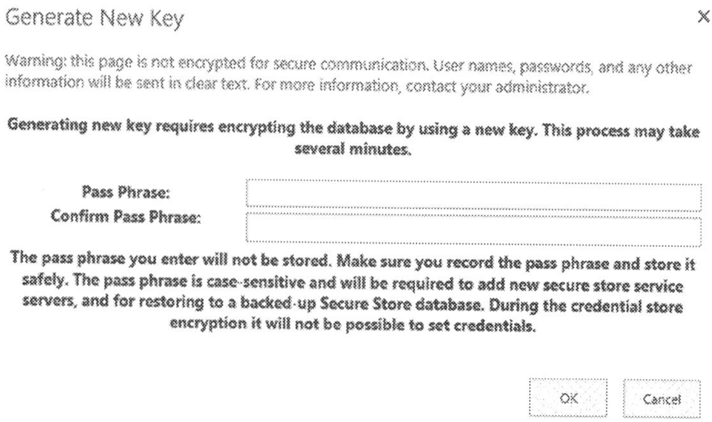

Generate New Key   ×

Warning: this page is not encrypted for secure communication. User names, passwords, and any other information will be sent in clear text. For more information, contact your administrator.

Generating new key requires encrypting the database by using a new key. This process may take several minutes.

      Pass Phrase: [   ]
Confirm Pass Phrase: [   ]

The pass phrase you enter will not be stored. Make sure you record the pass phrase and store it safely. The pass phrase is case-sensitive and will be required to add new secure store service servers, and for restoring to a backed-up Secure Store database. During the credential store encryption it will not be possible to set credentials.

                                    [OK]   [Cancel]

Figure 4-32. *The Generate New Key dialog*

- Refresh Key: To refresh a key (Figure 4-33), you again need Administrator rights, as well as the pass phrase you set when you created the key.

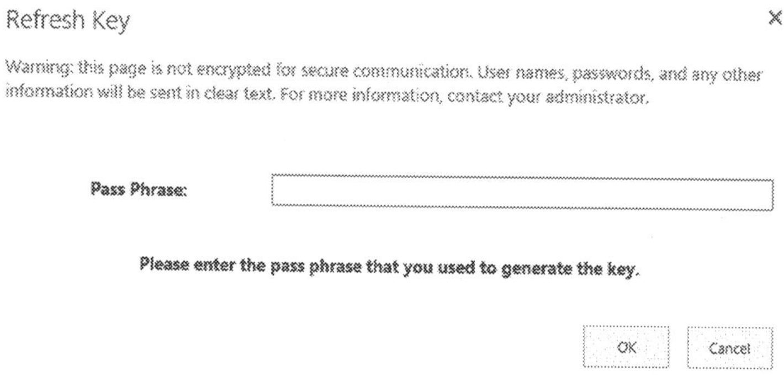

Refresh Key   ×

Warning: this page is not encrypted for secure communication. User names, passwords, and any other information will be sent in clear text. For more information, contact your administrator.

Pass Phrase: [   ]

Please enter the pass phrase that you used to generate the key.

                                    [OK]   [Cancel]

Figure 4-33. *Enter the pass phrase to refresh a key*

■ **Note** Refreshing a key will be necessary if you add a new application server to the existing server farm, or if you restore a secure store service database, or if you receive errors such as "Unable to get master key."

56

▓ **Caution**   Secure Store Services has its own database. Whenever you create a new key or refresh an existing key, be sure to back up the database.

4.   After you have successfully created the new key, click the New button under Manage Target Applications on the Edit tab of the ribbon and provide the following information in the Target Application Settings window.

- Target Application ID: A unique identifier that will be used in service applications as the unattended service account reference for authentication. Once created, you can't change the Target Application ID.

- Display Name: A name used for display purpose only.

- Contact E-mail: The primary email for this Application ID.

- Target Application Type: Specify Individual for individual users and Group for group credentials.

- Target Application Page URL: Selecting Use default page will use the sign-up page `http://yoursite/_layouts/SecureStoreSetCredentials.aspx?TargetAppId=<applicationId>`; this option is only available when you select the Individual Target Application Type. If you select Use custom page, you need to create a page first and provide its URL. This page is used to authenticate users. Choose None if you don't want a sign-up page.

5.   Enter VisioServices for the Target Application ID; SSS for Visio Services for the Display Name; <YourValidEmailAddress> for the Contact E-mail; Individual for the Target Application Type; Use default page for the Target Application Page URL (see Figure 4-34). Click Next.

Target Application Settings

The Secure Store Target Application ID is a unique identifier. You cannot change this property after you create the Target Application.

The display name is used for display purposes only.

The contact e-mail should be a valid e-mail address of the primary contact for this Target Application.

The Target Application type determines whether this application uses a group mapping or individual mapping. Ticketing indicates whether tickets are used for this Target Application. You cannot change this property after you create the Target Application.

The Target Application page URL can be used to set the values for the credential fields for the Target Application by individual users.

Target Application ID

    VisioServices

Display Name

    SSS for Visio Services

Contact E-mail

    srini@altsis.com

Target Application Type

    Individual   ▼

Target Application Page URL

⦿ Use default page
◯ Use custom page

◯ None

Next   Cancel

Figure 4-34. *Configuring target application settings for SSS*

6. In the Add Field window (Figure 4-35), leave the defaults as is and click on Next to continue.

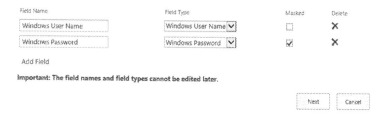

Field Name	Field Type	Masked	Delete
Windows User Name	Windows User Name ▼	☐	✕
Windows Password	Windows Password ▼	☑	✕

Add Field

Important: The field names and field types cannot be edited later.

Next   Cancel

Figure 4-35. *Secure Store Service fields*

7. Add administrator users who need to have access to this Application ID on the Target Application Administrators and click OK.

8. Return to the Secure Store Services window and choose the Target Application ID created in the previous step. Click the Set button on the Credentials tab of the Edit tab, as shown in Figure 4-36.

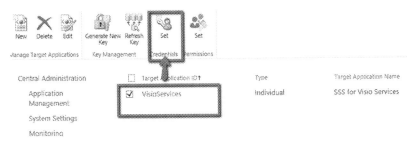

Figure 4-36. *Set Secure Store Service Application ID credentials*

9. On the Set Credentials for Secure Store Target Application screen (Figure 4-37), enter the Credential Owner, Windows user name and password (and confirm password), and click OK. Credential owners are the members (individuals or group) of the target application that will impersonate credentials when accessing external data.

Set Credentials for Secure Store Target Application (Individual)   ✕

Warning: this page is not encrypted for secure communication. User names, passwords, and any other information will be sent in clear text. For more information, contact your administrator.

Target Application Name: SSS for Visio Services

Target Application ID: VisioServices

Credential Owner:

Name	Value	Enter Windows User Name
Windows User Name		
Windows Password		
Confirm Windows Password		

Note: Once the credentials are set, they cannot be retrieved by the administrator. Any existing credentials for this credential owner will be overwritten.

OK   Cancel

Figure 4-37. *Setting credentials for target application*

▦ **Note**   Because you will be using SSS for your Visio diagram to connect to the SQL server, you will need to enter the user credentials of those who have permissions to the VisioServices database from where you will load data. It must be a low-privilege user, not an administrator.

The previous step creates a new SSS Application ID that can be used to connect to SQL Server from service applications that require additional authentication to retrieve data.

Using Visio with SQL Server and SSS

Now let's configure Visio Services to use the new Application ID:

1. Go to Central Administration ➤ Application Management ➤ Service Applications ➤ Manage Service Applications and choose Visio Graphics Service.

2. Click on the Global Settings in the External Data section and enter VisioServices under Application ID (Figure 4-38). Click OK.

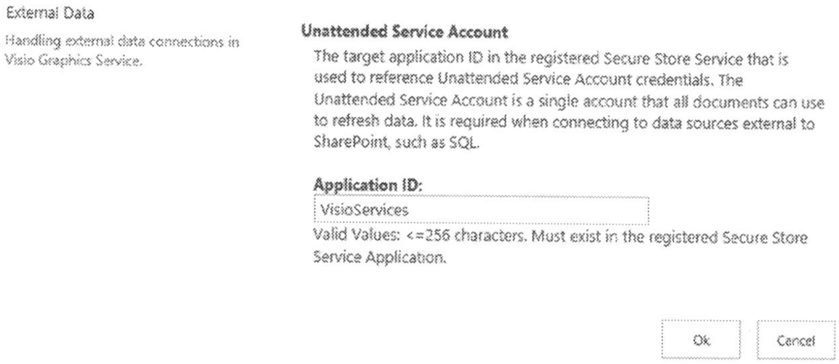

External Data

Handling external data connections in Visio Graphics Service.

Unattended Service Account

The target application ID in the registered Secure Store Service that is used to reference Unattended Service Account credentials. The Unattended Service Account is a single account that all documents can use to refresh data. It is required when connecting to data sources external to SharePoint, such as SQL.

Application ID:

VisioServices

Valid Values: <=256 characters. Must exist in the registered Secure Store Service Application.

Ok   Cancel

Figure 4-38. *Set the External Data Unattended Service Account Applicaion ID*

▦ **Note**   Application IDs are set for each service application, such as Visio Graphics Service. You can also have two Visio Graphics Service applications set for one Web application, one default and the other a Custom Visio Graphics service application. For that, create a new Application ID with different credentials and set them to a new Custom Service Application. You can then add the new custom service application to the web application Service Connections.

This sets the authorization proxy for the Visio Graphics Services to connect to the SQL Server database and retrieve data without losing the user context.

■ **Note**   Other settings on Visio Graphics Services under Global Settings include:

Maximum Web Drawing Size: This is the size of web drawing file that can be set, between 1 and 50 MB. The bigger the file size, the slower the rendering and performance.

Minimum Cache Age: This is the minimum duration in minutes each drawing is cached in memory. Set the value to zero if you need real-time data. However, setting this value to zero or too low puts a load on CPU and memory usage. The allowable range is 0–34560. This parameter is valid only for data-driven web drawings.

Maximum Cache Age: This is the value in minutes after which the cached drawings are removed from memory. You need to set this to zero (in addition to setting the Minimum Cache Age value to zero) to get real-time data. Setting this value too high will increase memory consumption but decreases file I/O and load on the CPU. This parameter is valid only for static web drawings.

Maximum Recalc Duration: This is the value in seconds of the period before an operation times out before a data refresh. The allowable range is between 10 and 120.

---

3. Open your SharePoint site and click on Mall.vsdx in the Visio Library document library to open the Visio diagram in full-screen mode.

4. Because you have set the SSS, data should display accurately from the database, with the data graphics populating the correct information on the shapes.

5. On SQL Server, go to the tblLandmarks table and change the data in the rows.

6. Return to the SharePoint site and refresh the Visio diagram to view the real-time changes in the diagram for the shapes, as shown in Figure 4-39.

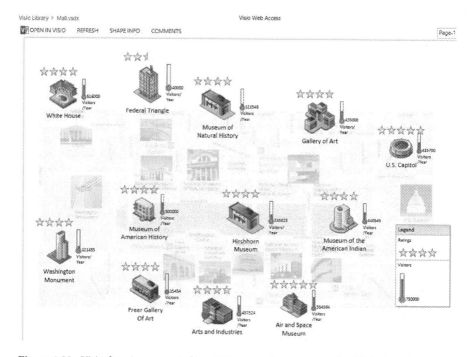

Figure 4-39. *Visio drawing connected to a SQL Server data source and published to SharePoint*

You can also interact with these Visio diagrams and shapes. For example, suppose that you want to get more information by clicking on a shape or to pass the information from a shape to another web part. You can achieve these scenarios by using the JavaScript API with Visio Services.

Visio Services JavaScript Mashup API

The Visio Services JavaScript Mashup API provides great functionality for accessing or manipulating the shapes of published diagrams. Using the API, you can alter data, shapes, and pages to make the diagrams more interactive. There are many operations you can perform on the drawings, some of which include:

- At the Control level, you can retrieve the version, display mode (Image), active page, and events such as shape selection changed, diagram render complete, and so on.

- At the Page level, you can get the available shapes, selected shape, shape, position, and other details.

- At the Shape Collection level, you can get the count, items, and metadata, and so on.

- At the Shape level, you can get the shape data and hyperlink, and set highlighting to the shape, overlays, and so on.

The Visio Services JavaScript Mashup API lets you create a rich user interface that combines shapes, data, and events.

The API consists of a hierarchy of classes, methods, and events, as shown in Figure 2-55. To obtain the reference of the Visio Web Access web part on a page you need to get the corresponding object, which can be accessed via the Vwa.VwaControl object. The next level would be the Page object.

■ **Note**   It is very important to understand that the page object in this context is the active web drawing page that is inside VWA web part—not the .aspx page.

On the page, you can have one or more shapes that can be retrieved using the ShapeCollection object. And, finally, you can access the individual shape from the shape collection and its properties.

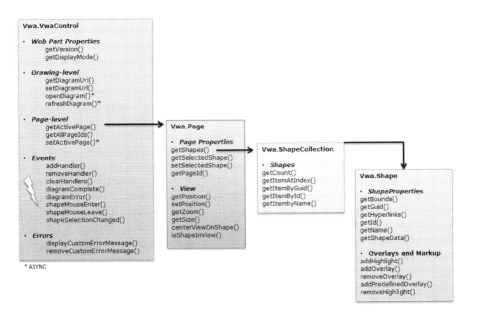

Figure 4-40. *Visio Services JavaScript Mashup API*

To use the JavaScript Mashup API and understand it more clearly, let's begin with a simple exercise.

PROBLEM CASE

Using the previously created Mall.vsdx, display the details of each monument by clicking the shape.

Solution

Create a new page under the site pages and name it Mall.aspx.

From Insert on the Editing Tools tab, under the Parts section, select Web Part and insert a Visio Web Access web part from the Business Data Categories. Add a web part to the page.

After you add the web part, make sure that the page is in edit mode and click the link that says Click here to open the tool pane.

From the Visio Web Access configuration window, choose Mall.vsdx from the Visio Library document library and click OK.

Click OK on the configuration window.

Save and close the page to view the Visio diagram rendered on the web page.

Right-click on the browser, click View Source on the context menu, and search for the text class="VisioWebAccess".

Find the corresponding id of the td that you should find just above the div. Usually it will be WebPartWPQ2 on a freshly created site page.

Open Notepad and paste the code in Listing 4-1 into it. Save this as the file assets.js.

Listing 4-1. Assets.js

```
<script language="javascript">
var _application = Sys.Application;
var _visioWebPart;
var onShapeSelectionChanged = null;
_application.add_load(onApplicationLoad);
function onApplicationLoad()
{
    _visioWebPart= new Vwa.VwaControl("WebPartWPQ2"); // Change the
    control id based on the code on your page
    _visioWebPart.addHandler("diagramcomplete", onDiagramComplete);
    _visioWebPart.addHandler("shapeselectionchanged",
    onShapeSelectionChanged);
}
```

```
function onDiagramComplete()
{
    var _page = _visioWebPart.getActivePage();
    _page.setZoom(85);
}
onShapeSelectionChanged = function(source, args)
{
    var _activePage = _visioWebPart.getActivePage();
    var _shape = _activePage.getShapes();
    var _shapeItem = _shape.getItemById(args);
    var _shapeData = _shapeItem.getShapeData();
    var _description = "";

    for (var j = 0; j < _shapeData.length; j++)
    {
        if (_shapeData[j].label == "Details")
        {
            _description = _shapeData[j].value;
            continue;
        }
    }
    document.getElementById('landmarkDetails').firstChild.data =
    _description;
}
</SCRIPT>
<div id="landmarkDetails" style="font-family: Verdana; font-style:
bold; font-size:14pt; color:red;">landmark details...</div>
```

Upload the assets.js file into the Visio Library document library.

Right-click on assets.js and, by using the Copy Shortcut menu, copy the URL to the clipboard.

Open the Mall.aspx site page in edit mode and add the Content Editor Web part from the Media and Content category, as shown in Figure 4-41.

Figure 4-41. *Adding the Content Editor web part to the page*

Edit the Content Editor Web part and paste the link to assets.js in the Content Link textbox.

Verify the link by clicking on Test link URL below the textbox. If the URL is accurate, the assets.js file will be downloaded to your disk.

Click Apply and OK on the editor part pane to return the page to normal mode.

Save and close the page.

You should now see that the Content Editor Web part displays "landmark details..." text in red, as shown in Figure 4-42.

Content Editor
landmark details...

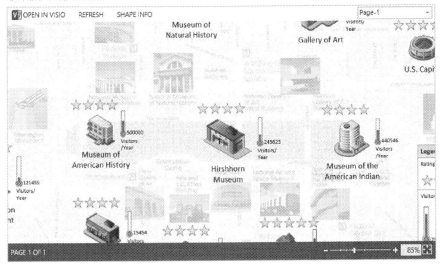

Figure 4-42. *The Cntent Editor web part with the Visio Web Access web part*

Click on any shape—for instance, on the White House—and see that the text on the Content Editor web part changes to the White House details, as shown in Figure 4-43. Try clicking on other shapes. Notice that the text changes on the Content Editor Web part instantly without a page refresh.

Content Editor

The White House is the official residence and principal workplace of the President of the United States. Located at 1600 Pennsylvania Avenue NW in Washington, D.C., it was designed by Irish-born James Hoban,[1] and built between 1792 and 1800 of white-painted Aquia sandstone in the late Georgian style. It has been the residence of every U.S. President since John Adams. When Thomas Jefferson moved into the home in 1801, he (with architect Benjamin Henry Latrobe) expanded the building outward, creating two colonnades that were meant to conceal stables and storage

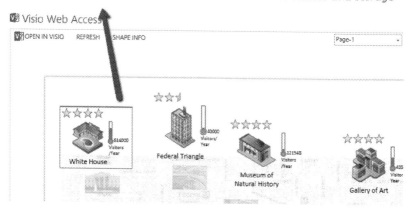

Figure 4-43. *Interacting with the VWA web part and the drawing using the JavaScript Mashup API*

Now that you have successfully created a simple JavaScript mashup with a Visio diagram, let's understand the code. One of the major reasons that JavaScript was chosen to build the API is because of its simplicity.

Understanding the assets.js Code

First, we need to get to the application object and create the event handler for the application load:

```
_application.add_load(onApplicationLoad);
```

Once the application loads, we get the instance of the Visio web access from the page and add two more event handlers—one when the diagram completes loading and the other when the shape selection is changed. In the life cycle of these events, the onDiagramComplete event fires first, and onShapeSelectionChanged is the last event:

```
_visioWebPart= new Vwa.VwaControl("WebPartWPQ2");
_visioWebPart.addHandler("diagramcomplete", onDiagramComplete);
_visioWebPart.addHandler("shapeselectionchanged", onShapeSelectionChanged);
```

After the diagram loads, all of the objects are available and the diagram is rendered to the browser. This means that the diagram is completely available on the page and we can get to the page-level properties and methods. For example, we can set the diagram current page zoom value percentage:

```
var _page = _visioWebPart.getActivePage();
_page.setZoom(85);
```

Once any shape is selected or changed on the active page, we need the corresponding shape and the shape data. We need to get to Shape Data in order to get the column values. We use the method getItemById(), which is submitted through the event arguments:

```
var _activePage = _visioWebPart.getActivePage();
var _shape = _activePage.getShapes();
var _shapeItem = _shape.getItemById(args);
var _shapeData = _shapeItem.getShapeData();
var _description = "";
for (var j = 0; j < _shapeData.length; j++)
    {
      if (_shapeData[j].label == "Details"){
            _description = _shapeData[j].value;
            continue;
        }
    }
```

Finally, we get the description and assign it to the div text:

```
document.getElementById('landmarkDetails').firstChild.data = _description;
```

Now, suppose that your business analyst wants to create a simple workflow using a Visio diagram? Is there a way to connect this diagram to one of the available workflows easily?

Working with SharePoint Designer 2013

The answer to the questions in previous sections is yes! These scenarios can be achieved using Visio 2013 diagrams with SharePoint Designer 2013, which now allows importing and exporting Visio diagrams, attaching workflows to them, and then publishing to SharePoint environment. A big difference between SharePoint 2010 style workflows and SharePoint 2013 style workflows is that Visio visualizations are supported only on SharePoint 2010 style workflows.

```
┌──────────────────────────────────────────────────────────────┐
│                        PROBLEM CASE                            │
└──────────────────────────────────────────────────────────────┘
```

One of the leading fast food chains (let's call it "Tasty Foods") wants to collect feedback from its customers on various food items. The feedback form must be filled out by the customer using an online web application. Customers must enter their full name, food item, and email address, and they must leave comments. If the customer doesn't enter a comment, the workflow status will be rejected; if he does, the status will be approved.

There are three major components that will be used in this case:

- A SharePoint list, used as the feedback form (responsibility of the developer).

- A Visio diagram to create the workflow design (responsibility of the business analyst).

- SharePoint Designer to enable the workflow and deploy (attach) it to the list (responsibility of the developer).

Solution

Create a custom list, add a few columns as shown in Figure 4-44, and save it as Tasty Foods Feedback.

Columns

A column stores information about each item in the list. The following columns are currently available in this list:

Column (click to edit)	Type	Required
Title	Single line of text	✔
Full Name	Single line of text	
FoodItem	Choice	
Email Address	Single line of text	
Comments	Multiple lines of text	
Created By	Person or Group	
Modified By	Person or Group	

Figure 4-44. *The Tasty Foods custom list*

The Fooditem Choice column can contain items such as Sandwiches, Chicken Burger, Breakfast, Salads, Snacks and Sides, Beverages, Coffee, Desserts, Shakes, and so on.

Open Visio 2013 and create a new Visio diagram using Shape Stencils SharePoint Workflow Actions (US units). You'll find these in the Flowchart section.

Create a simple workflow as shown in Figure 4-45, using shapes that compare the data source, send email, and set the workflow status.

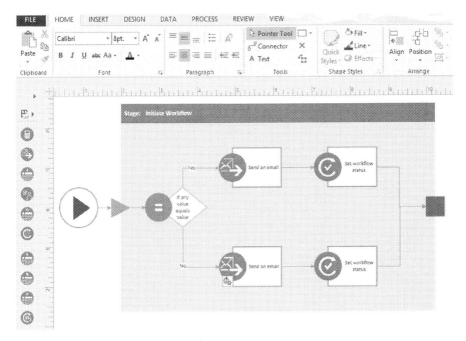

Figure 4-45. *Simple workflow designed in Visio using SharePoint templates*

From the File menu, save the diagram (as a .vsdx file) to your local file system.

Close the file and open the SharePoint Designer 2013 client.

Open the SharePoint site where you created the Tasty Foods Feedback custom list.

From the Site Objects menu, click on Workflows.

On the Workflow tab of the ribbon under Manage section, click on the Import from Visio icon dropdown and choose 'Import Visio 2013 diagram', as shown in Figure 4-46.

Figure 4-46. *Import Visio 2013 Diagram*

In the 'Import workflow from Visio drawing' window, browse and select the previously created .vsxd file, then click Open to continue, as shown in Figure 4-47.

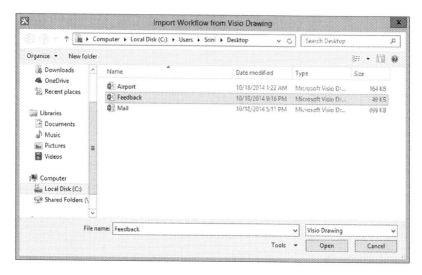

Figure 4-47. *Importing a Visio workflow interchange file to SharePoint Designer*

Under the 'Create Workflow' window, provide a proper workflow name and choose List Workflow as the type of workflow to import. Select the custom list you created earlier for the feedback and click Finish, as shown in Figure 4-48.

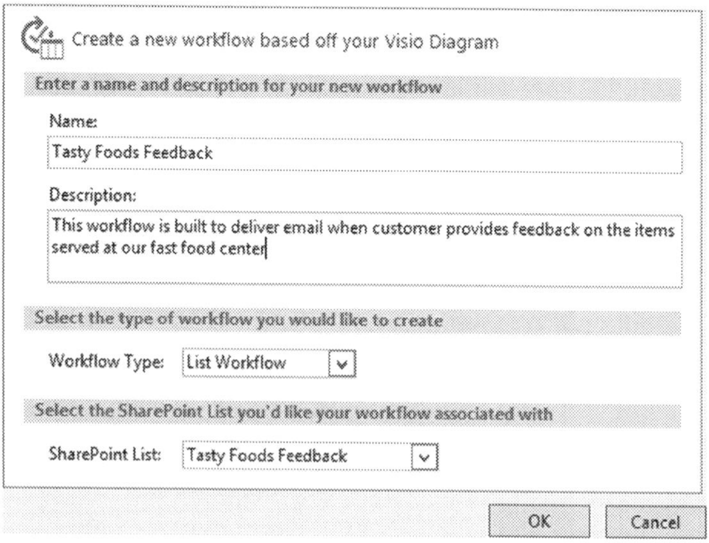

Figure 4-48. *Setting the workflow name and selecting the list to attach to the workflow*

This opens the workflow in Visual Designer view, as shown in Figure 4-49.

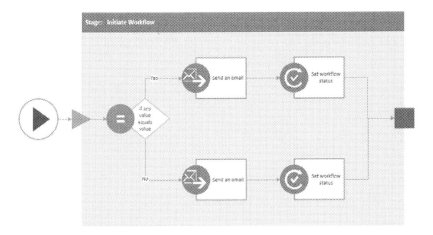

Figure 4-49. *Visio Designer View*

This feature is new in SharePoint Designer 2013. However, you can toggle between Text-Based and Visual designer by selecting the choices under 'Views' button, as shown in Figure 4-50.

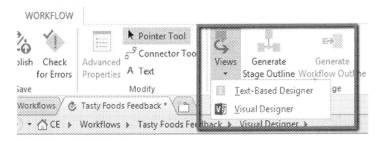

Figure 4-50. *Visio workflow intechange file (.vwi) loaded in the SharePoint Designer workflow editor*

▓ **Note**　This feature is available only when both SharePoint Designer and Visio 2013 clients are installed on same machine.

Once you switch to Text-Based designer, two conditions are automatically created under the editor as there are two flows when comparing the data (refer to Figure 4-51). This includes the send email process step, change the workflow status, and the end the process step for both flows.

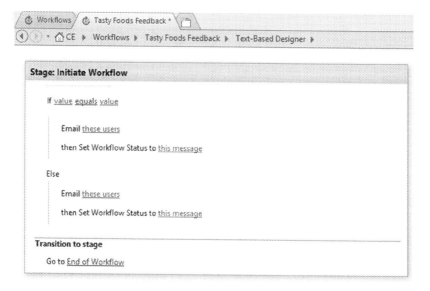

Figure 4-51. *Visio Text-Based View*

Set the value to look up from the custom list data source and choose the field (Comments) for looking up the value. Set the Operator value to "is empty" and click OK.

If this condition is true, then set the Email "these users" to Current Item:Email Address. Configure Subject and message and then set workflow status to "Rejected" from the lookup values.

Under the "Else" condition, set Email "these users" to Current Item:Email Address. Configure Subject and message and then Set workflow to "Approved".

Finally, set the Title of the workflow as "Tasty Foods Feedback Workflow", as shown in Figure 4-52.

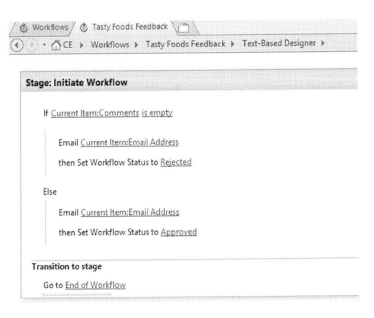

Figure 4-52. *Setting up the workflow conditions in SharePoint Designer*

In the Start Options, under View and manage settings for this workflow page, you can choose to start the workflow automatically either when the item is created or when it is changed (see Figure 4-53).

Figure 4-53. *Setting workflow startup options in SharePoint Designer*

From the Workflow tab on the ribbon, click the Check for Errors button and then save the workflow (Figure 4-54).

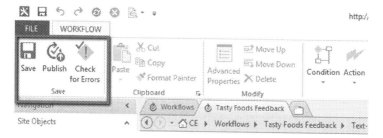

Figure 4-54. *Save and Publish the workflow to SharePoint list*

Publish this workflow to the list using the Publish button on the Workflow tab.

These steps will validate and publish the workflow to the corresponding list:

Open the SharePoint site and the Tasty Foods Feedback list.

Go to List ➤ List Settings and click on the Workflow Settings in the Permissions and Management section. You can also access the Workflow settings from List Tools ➤ List ➤ Settings ➤ Workflow Settings.

Locate the Workflow that you just submitted. If the workflow is published more than once, a new version is created.

Return to the list and click Add new item, which pops up the New Item screen, as shown in Figure 4-55.

Title *	
Full Name	
FoodItem	Sandwiches
Email Address	
Comments	

Save   Cancel

Figure 4-55. *Adding a new item to the feedback form*

Create two items, one with comments and one without comments. Because the workflow hasn't been set to start automatically, you'll have to start it manually after any item is created. Choose the item on which you'd like to run the Workflow and click the Workflows button on the Items tab, as shown in Figure 4-56.

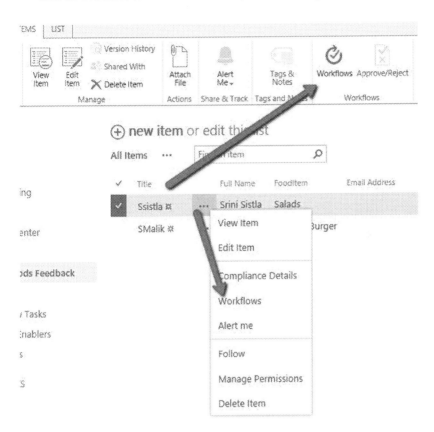

Figure 4-56. *Starting a workflow for the list item*

This opens the Start a New Workflow window, displaying the available workflows, as shown in Figure 4-57.

Figure 4-57. *Starting a new workflow*

Click on the Tasty Foods Feedback workflow link, and then on the Start button on the next screen. This will execute the rules underlying the workflow and apply any changes to the respective columns.

Notice that under the Tasty Foods Feedback column (Figure 4-58), the status is set based the on the comments provided by customer. The status would be Approved when the customer fills in the Comments field and Rejected when the customer doesn't add any comments.

Figure 4-58. *Workflow status after items are added*

In some instances, the requirement may not be as simple as just connecting to an Excel file or SharePoint list or even using a SQL Server database. A more interesting scenario would be consuming data from a web service or from a different data source that Visio Services doesn't support natively. In such cases, you would have to write a custom data provider.

Creating Your Own Custom Data Providers

The Visio Services API provides features to build custom data modules or custom data providers. Using the API, you can create custom data sources and refresh the data on the Visio diagrams that are deployed to a SharePoint site.

▧ **Note**   Custom data providers cannot be used with SharePoint Online sites.

Let's take a look now at how to support non-natively supported data sources by designing a custom data provider.

```
                            PROBLEM CASE
```

Display the status of the test environment servers whether they are online or offline. Notice that current status information is in a SQL Server database and can be retrieved using WCF services. We will need to get the data and connect to the shapes.

Solution

The major components in this scenario are SQL Server, WCF Service, Visio, and Security.

Let's begin with a SQL Server database and then write a WCF Service to retrieve data from the database table.

We'll write a VBA script to create the data source and connect the data source to the shapes in the Visio diagram.

We'll deploy the .vsdx file to a SharePoint environment and view the output.

We'll write a custom data provider and configure its settings in the Central Administration site of the SharePoint environment.

Create a table named tblServerStatus with columns, as shown in Figure 4-59, in the VisioServices database that you created earlier.

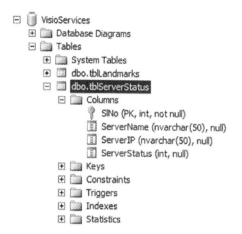

Figure 4-59. *Server Status Table in SQL Server*

Populate a few rows of information into this table, as shown in Figure 4-60.

	SINo	ServerName	ServerIP	ServerStatus
▶	1	WEBWASDC01	192.168.2.1	1
	2	WEBWASDC02	192.168.2.2	1
	3	APPWASDC01	192.168.2.3	0
*	NULL	NULL	NULL	NULL

Figure 4-60. *Populating data for the server status table in SQL Server*

Create a stored procedure named uspGetServerDetails that will execute the SQL query to retrieve the values from the table in Figure 4-59. Listing 4-2 shows the code.

Listing 4-2. The uspGetServerDetails Stored Procedure

```
USE [VisioServices]
GO
/****** Object:  StoredProcedure [dbo].[uspGetServerDetails]
Script Date: 10/18/2014 11:30:11 PM ******/
SET ANSI_NULLS ON
GO
SET QUOTED_IDENTIFIER ON
GO
```

```
-- ===============================================
-- Author:                 <Author,,Name>
-- Create date: <Create Date,,>
-- Description:            <Description,,>
-- ===============================================
CREATE PROCEDURE [dbo].[uspGetServerDetails]
AS
BEGIN
        -- SET NOCOUNT ON added to prevent extra result sets from
        -- interfering with SELECT statements.
        SET NOCOUNT ON;
    -- Insert statements for procedure here
        SELECT ServerName, ServerIP, ServerStatus from
tblServerStatus
END
```

■ **Note**   The stored procedure code is explained toward the end of this chapter in the section "Understanding the Custom Data Provider Code."

Writing the WCF Service library and Hosting it in IIS

Open Microsoft Visual Studio 2013, choose to create a new project, and from the available templates select Visual C# ➤ WCF ➤ WCF Service Application, and provide a proper Name and Location. Make sure that you pick .NET Framework 3.5. This creates a service class (Service1.svc) and an interface (IService1.cs).

Rename the default Service1.svc file and the interface class to ServerStatus.svc and IServerStatus.cs, respectively. Ensure that all of the references under the project reflect this name change.

After completing these steps, your project should look like the one in Figure 4-61.

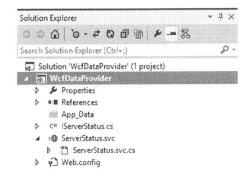

Figure 4-61. *Setting up a WCF service application project in Visual Studio 2013*

Open the Web.config file and add an entry under the `connectionStrings` section—
your SQL Server connection string as follows:

```
<connectionStrings>
    <add name="VisioServicesConnectionString" connectionString="Data
Source=ServerName;Initial Catalog=VisioServices;Integrated
Security=SSPI;User Id=userId;Password=pwd" providerName="System.Data.
SqlClient"/>
    </connectionStrings>
```

Open the ServerStatus.svc.cs file and paste the code from Listing 4-3 in it.

▨ **Note**   The code in Listing 4-3 is explained toward the end of this chapter in the section
"Understanding the Custom Data provider code."

Listing 4-3. WCF Service Library class to retreive Server Status

```
using System;
using System.Collections.Generic;
using System.Linq;
using System.Runtime.Serialization;
using System.ServiceModel;
using System.Text;
using System.Data;
using System.Data.Sql;
using System.Data.SqlClient;
using System.Configuration;
namespace WcfDataProvider
{
    public class ServerStatus : IServerStatus
    {
        [OperationBehavior]
        public DataTable GetServerStatusDetails()
        {
            DataSet dataSet = new DataSet();
            SqlConnection connection = new SqlConnection(Configuration
            Manager.ConnectionStrings["VisioServicesConnectionString"].
            ConnectionString);

            SqlCommand command = new SqlCommand("uspGetServerDetails",
            connection);
            command.CommandType = CommandType.StoredProcedure;
            SqlDataAdapter dataAdapter = new SqlDataAdapter(command);
```

```
            dataAdapter.Fill(dataSet);
            connection.Close();
            return dataSet.Tables[0];
        }
    }
}
```

Now copy the code in Listing 4-4, open the IServerStatus.cs file, and paste the code in it.

■ **Best Practice**   It is good practice to add a Test Project for any projects you create as this would perform the first level of unit testing.

Listing 4-4. WCF Service library Interface Class

```
using System;
using System.Collections.Generic;
using System.Linq;
using System.Runtime.Serialization;
using System.ServiceModel;
using System.Text;
using System.Data;
namespace WcfDataProvider
{
    // NOTE: You can use the "Rename" command on the "Refactor" menu
    to change the interface name "IServerStatus" in both code and config
    file together.
    [ServiceContract]
    public interface IServerStatus
    {
        [OperationContract]
        DataTable GetServerStatusDetails();
    }
}
```

Build the WCF project in release mode and make sure that there are no errors.

Create a local folder in your file system under C:\ and name it wcfServicehost.

Make a folder called bin.

Copy the WcfDataProvider.dll file to the bin folder.

Make sure that Network Service and IIS_IUSRS users have Read & Execute permissions on the root folder.

Create a file named VisioWcfService.svc under the wcfServicehost folder and add
the following text:

```
<% @ServiceHost Service="WcfDataProvider.ServerStatus" %>
```

Create a Web.config file in the same folder and copy the code from Listing 4-5 to it.

Listing 4-5. WCF data provider Web.config file settings

```
<?xml version="1.0" encoding="utf-8"?>
  <configuration>
    <system.serviceModel>
      <services>
        <service behaviorConfiguration="WcfDataProvider.
        ServerStatusBehavior" name="WcfDataProvider.ServerStatus">
          <endpoint address="" binding="basicHttpBinding"
          contract="WcfDataProvider.IServerStatus" />
                    <host>
              <baseAddresses>
                <add baseAddress="http://localhost:<portnumber>/
                                   visiowcfservices.svc" />
              </baseAddresses>
            </host>
        </service>
      </services>
      <behaviors>
        <serviceBehaviors>
          <behavior name="WcfDataProvider.ServerStatusBehavior">
            <serviceMetadata httpGetEnabled="true" />
            <serviceDebug includeExceptionDetailInFaults="false" />
          </behavior>
        </serviceBehaviors>
      </behaviors>
    </system.serviceModel>
    <connectionStrings>
      <add name="VisioServicesConnectionString"
connectionString="Data Source=ServerName;Initial Catalog=Visi
oServices;Integrated Security=SSPI;User Id=uid;Password=pwd"
providerName="System.Data.SqlClient"/>
    </connectionStrings>
  </configuration>
```

After completing these steps, your folder structure and files should look similar to
those shown in Figure 4-62.

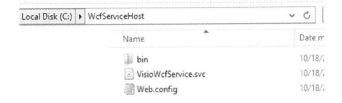

Figure 4-62. *WCF service host folder*

Open IIS and create an application pool by providing a Name, .NET Framework version, and pipeline mode.

Create a new website. Choose the app pool that you just created, provide a site name, and choose the local folder where you copied the .dll file as the physical path. Under binding, provide a Port number that's not in use.

Open the browser and type the URL `http://localhost:<portnumber>/VisioWcfServices.svc;` to see the output shown in Figure 4-63.

ServerStatus Service

You have created a service.

To test this service, you will need to create a client and use it to call the service. You can do this using the svcutil.exe following syntax:

```
svcutil.exe http://sp.ce.int:1900/VisioWcfService.svc?wsdl
```

You can also access the service description as a single file:

```
http://sp.ce.int:1900/VisioWcfService.svc?singleWsdl
```

This will generate a configuration file and a code file that contains the client class. Add the two files to your client appl call the Service. For example:

C#

```
class Test
{
    static void Main()
    {
        ServerStatusClient client = new ServerStatusClient();

        // Use the 'client' variable to call operations on the service.

        // Always close the client.
        client.Close();
    }
}
```

Visual Basic

```
Class Test
    Shared Sub Main()
        Dim client As ServerStatusClient = New ServerStatusClient()
        ' Use the 'client' variable to call operations on the service.

        ' Always close the client.
        client.Close()
    End Sub
End Class
```

Figure 4-63. *Accessing the WCF service*

> ■ **Note** For more information on how to create WCF services, go to
> `http://blah.winsmarts.com/2008-4-Host_a_WCF_Service_in_IIS_7_-and-amp;`
> `_Windows_2008_-_The_right_way.aspx`.

Creating the custom data provider project

Open Microsoft Visual Studio 2013, create a new project, and from the available templates pick Visual C# ➤ Office/SharePoint ➤ SharePoint Solutions ➤ SharePoint 2013 - Empty SharePoint Project. Make sure you choose .NET Framework 4.5. Provide a Name, Location, and Solution Name, and click OK. Create the project name as VisioDataService.

In the next screen, enter the SharePoint site URL for debugging and choose Deploy as a farm solution for the trust level. Click on Finish.

Right-click on the project, select the properties, and make sure that the Assembly name and default namespace fit your situation.

Right-click on the project again and click on Add Class. Name the class as VisioDataService.cs.

Right-click on the project and choose Add Service Reference...

From the wizard, click Discover and make sure there's a reference to the WCF service you built earlier. Alternatively, you can enter the WCF URL (`http://localhost:<portnumber>/VisioWcfServices.svc`) in the Address text box. Provide the namespace as WcfDataService and click OK.

Right-click on the project and choose Add Reference... From the Add Reference window .NET tab, choose the System.Web component and click OK.

Right-click on the project again and choose Add Reference... From the Add Reference window Browse tab, browse to the folder : `\Windows\assembly\GAC_MSIL\Microsoft.Office.Visio.Server\14.0.0.0__71e9bce111e9429c\` and choose the file Microsoft.Office.Visio.Server.dll and click OK.

At this stage, the project structure should resemble the one shown in Figure 4-64.

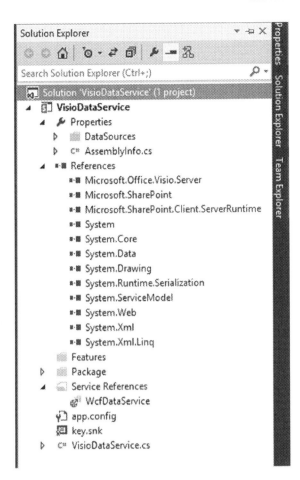

Figure 4-64. *WCF consumer project structure*

Open the VisioDataService.cs file from the VisioDataService project and copy the code in Listing 4-6 into the file. Make sure that you have the correct namespaces as per your project settings.

Listing 4-6. Visio Custom Data Provider Service Class Code

```
using System;
using System.Data;
using System.Threading;
using System.Xml;
using System.Web;
using Microsoft.Office.Visio.Server;
using VisioDataService.WcfDataService;
namespace Altsis
```

```
{
    public class VisioDataService : AddonDataHandler, IAsyncResult
    {
        private object _asyncState;
        private bool _completeStatus;
        WaitHandle IAsyncResult.AsyncWaitHandle
        {
            get { return null; }
        }
        object IAsyncResult.AsyncState
        {
            get { return _asyncState; }
        }
        bool IAsyncResult.IsCompleted
        {
            get { return this._completeStatus; }
        }
        bool IAsyncResult.CompletedSynchronously
        {
            get { return false; }
        }
        public override IAsyncResult BeginGetData(HttpContext
        httpContext, AsyncCallback callback, object asyncState)
        {
            _asyncState = asyncState;
            ThreadPool.QueueUserWorkItem(new WaitCallback(GetData),
            callback);
            return this;
        }
        public override DataSet EndGetData(IAsyncResult asyncResult)
        {
            return this.Data;
        }
        public override void Cancel()
        {
            // Not implemented
        }
        private void GetData(object state)
        {
            AsyncCallback asyncCallback = (AsyncCallback)state;
            try
            {
                ServerStatusClient oServerStatus = new ServerStatusClient();
                    DataTable dt = oServerStatus.GetServerStatusDetails();
                this.Data.Reset();
                this.Data.Tables.Add(dt);
                this.Data.AcceptChanges();
            }
```

```
        catch (Exception ex)
        {
            this.Error = new AddonDataHandlerException(ex.Message);
        }
        asyncCallback(this);
        _completeStatus = true;
    }
  }
}
```

■ **Note** The code in Listing 4-6 is explained toward the end of this chapter in the section "Understanding the Custom Data provider code."

Now build the project. Once the build is successful, right-click on the VisioDataService project, then click on 'Publish...'. Choose target location and publish the WSP file.

■ **Tip** If you are performing this step on your local development machine, try the Deploy option from the project properties.

Deploy the WSP using either STSADM or Windows PowerShell commands to add the solution to your SharePoint site.

Open Central Administration ➤ Application Management ➤ Manage Service Applications ➤ Visio Graphics Service.

Click on Trusted Data Providers and then on Add a new Trusted Data Provider.

Under Trusted Data Provider ID, enter the fully qualified assembly signature (in my case, it is Altsis.VisioDataService,VisioDataService, Version=1.0.0.0, Culture=neutral, PublicKeyToken=<publickeytoken>). Please see http://blah.winsmarts.com/2009-12-SharePoint_Productivity_Tip_of_the_day.aspx for a convenient way to extract assembly signatures.

Under Trusted Data Provider Type, enter the value 6 (for Visio Custom Data Providers).

Under Trusted Data Provider Description, enter a valid description such as Visio Custom Data Services Provider and click OK.

Your service provider is now ready and will display in the available service provider list.

Open the Web.config file that belongs to your SharePoint web application and paste the code in Listing 4-7 under the system.serviceModel section.

Listing 4-7. Service Model section setting values under web.config file

```
<bindings>
    <basicHttpBinding>
        <binding name="BasicHttpBinding_IServerStatus" closeTimeout="00:01:00"
            openTimeout="00:01:00" receiveTimeout="00:10:00"
            sendTimeout="00:01:00"
            allowCookies="false" bypassProxyOnLocal="false" hostNameC
            omparisonMode="StrongWildcard"
            maxBufferSize="65536" maxBufferPoolSize="524288"
            maxReceivedMessageSize="65536"
            messageEncoding="Text" textEncoding="utf-8"
            transferMode="Buffered"
            useDefaultWebProxy="true">
            <readerQuotas maxDepth="32" maxStringContentLength="8192"
            maxArrayLength="16384"
                maxBytesPerRead="4096" maxNameTableCharCount="16384" />
            <security mode="None">
                <transport clientCredentialType="None" proxyCredentialType="None"
                    realm="" />
                <message clientCredentialType="UserName" algorithmSuite="Default" />
            </security>
        </binding>
    </basicHttpBinding>
</bindings>
<client>
    <endpoint address="http://varun.altsis.com:77/VisioWcfServices.svc"
        binding="basicHttpBinding" bindingConfiguration="BasicHttpB
        inding_IServerStatus"
        contract="WcfDataService.IServerStatus"
        name="BasicHttpBinding_IServerStatus" />
</client>
```

Designing the Visio Diagram

Open Visio 2013 and create a blank diagram. Choose the Network ➤ Servers (US units) stencil from More Shapes ➤ Network.

From the Insert tab, add a Container block from the diagram parts, and add three servers: Web Server, Database Server, and Application Server. Give a name to the Container block, as shown in Figure 4-65.

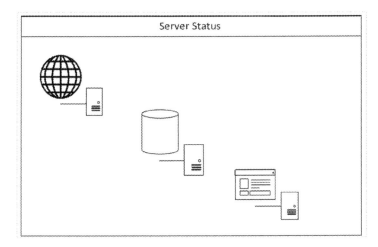

Figure 4-65. *Designing a Visio diagram for test servers*

Right now, there is no data source configured. While your Visio diagram is open, press Alt+F11 to open Microsoft Visual Basic for Applications. In the Project window, double-click on ThisDocument under Visio Objects to open the code view. Paste the code in Listing 4-8 into the code area.

Listing 4-8. Using Visual Basic for applications to retreive data from SQL Server data source

```
Sub LoadData()
    Dim diagramServices As Integer
    Dim vsoDataRecordset As Visio.dataRecordset

    Dim connectionString As String
    Dim commandText As String

    diagramServices = ActiveDocument.DiagramServicesEnabled
    ActiveDocument.DiagramServicesEnabled = visServiceVersion140
    Application.ActiveWindow.Windows.ItemFromID(visWinIDExternalData)
    .Visible = True

    commandText = "SELECT ServerName, ServerIP, ServerStatus FROM
    tblServerStatus"
    connectionString = "Provider=SQLOLEDB;Data Source=<YourDataSource
    Name>;Initial Catalog=VisioServices;Integrated Security=SSPI;"
    Set vsoDataRecordset = ActiveDocument.DataRecordsets.
    Add(connectionString, commandText, 0, "Server Status Details")
```

```
vsoDataRecordset.DataConnection.connectionString =
"DataModule=Altsis.VisioDataService,VisioDataService;"

ActiveDocument.DiagramServicesEnabled = diagramServices
End Sub
```

░ **Note**　The code in Listing 4-8 is explained toward the end of this chapter in the section "Understanding the Custom Data provider code." You will need to customize the connection string and the Data module assembly details in the code.

The Microsoft Visual Basic for Applications window should look like the one shown in Figure 4-66.

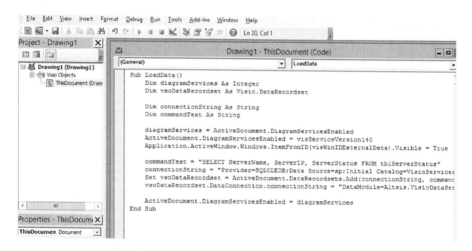

Figure 4-66. *Microsoft Visual Basic for Applications*

Press F5 or click on the Run button on the menu to execute the LoadData() subroutine. Pressing Alt+F11 will toggle back to the Visio diagram. Under the External Data tab, the data will be loaded, as shown in Figure 4-67.

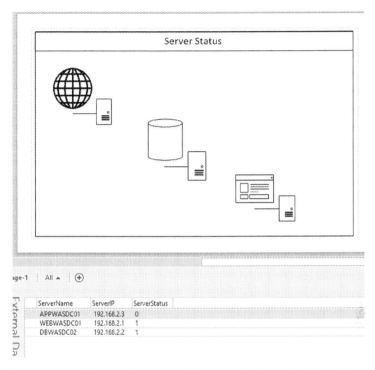

Figure 4-67. *The Visio diagram loading external data using VBA code*

Drag and drop row data to the respective shapes or set the Text property to the shapes that match the ServerName column and use the option Automatically Link all.

Set the data graphics to display ServerIP and ServerName as Text, and ServerStatus as Color by Value (Figure 4-68), such that if the value is 0 (server is down) the server shows red and if the value is 1 (server is live), it show green.

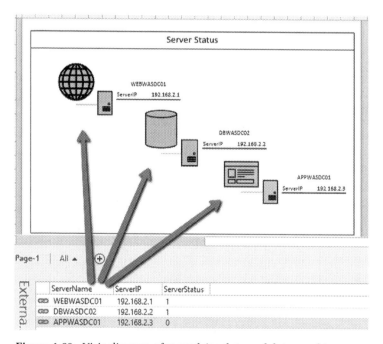

Figure 4-68. *Setting up Data Graphics for the Visio diagram*

Your final Visio diagram before saving should look like the one shown in Figure 4-69.

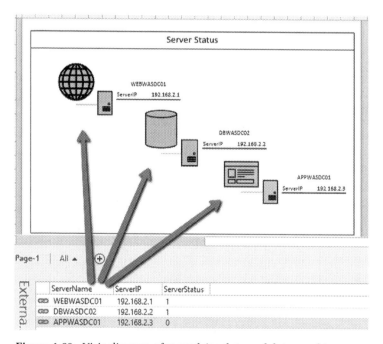

Figure 4-69. *Visio diagram after applying data and data graphics*

Save the Visio diagram to the local file system.

From the File menu, click on Save & Send ➤ Save to SharePoint ➤ Web Drawing ➤ Save As .vdw file.

Note VSDX file does not support macros. Hence, you will have to save the file as .vdw and use it in SharePoint 2013.

Open the SharePoint site and open the Visio Library Document library. Click on Add document, browse to the saved .vdw file, and click OK.

Click on the .vsdx file to open the diagram in the browser to display the results from the database.

Change the values in the database and notice the server status. If the cache age values on the general settings of the Visio Graphics Service are set to zero, the values reflect instantly on the diagram (Figure 4-70).

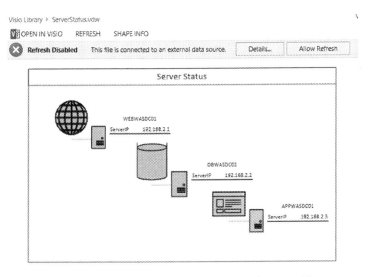

Figure 4-70. Visio diagram loaded using a custom data provider

Make sure that the following are correct to avoid the error shown in Figure 4-71:

Figure 4-71. External data connection refresh error

Assembly details are accurate when you add the custom data providers in the Central Administration.

The WCF services are properly hosted and can communicate with the Custom Data Providers.

Your configuration files (Web.config) have the right binding settings for the WCF. As discussed earlier, you might encounter the double-hop issue while connecting to data sources via WCF. If so, you might need to set the credentials under the Secure Store Service.

Understanding the Custom Data Provider Code

This section provides some more details on the code listings given earlier.

uspGetServerDetails Stored Procedure (Listing 4-2)

This stored procedure contains a simple T-SQL statement that retrieves all rows of data from the table tblServerStatus.

```
SELECT ServerName, ServerIP, ServerStatus from tblServerStatus
```

WCF Service Library (and Interface) Class (Listings 4-3 and 4-4):

Consider this a data access layer class that would call the uspGetServerDetails stored procedure and return the output as a data table.

When the WCF application project is created, a service class and corresponding interface template are added to the project. Declare the Service Contract and Operation Contract (as shown below) interface class that will be implemented in your derived class. Because the intention is to retrieve a data table from this service, the data contract method will be of type DataTable:

```
[ServiceContract]
    public interface IServerStatus
    {
        [OperationContract]
        DataTable GetServerStatusDetails();
    }
```

Under the derived class in the implemented method GetServerStatusDetails, create the data objects needed for the output:

```
DataSet dataSet = new DataSet();
```

Next, create the SQL Connection using the connection string from Web.config:

```
SqlConnection connection = new SqlConnection(ConfigurationManager.Connection
Strings["VisioServicesConnectionString"].ConnectionString);
```

Create the command object by calling the stored procedure with the help of the SQL Connection and set the command type to StoredProcedure:

```
SqlCommand command = new SqlCommand("uspGetServerDetails", connection);
command.CommandType = CommandType.StoredProcedure;
```

Finally, create the data adapter, load the command, and fill the data set using the data adapter:

```
SqlDataAdapter dataAdapter = new SqlDataAdapter(command);
dataAdapter.Fill(dataSet);
```

Close the connection and return the output:

```
connection.Close();
return dataSet.Tables[0];
```

▨ **Tip**   If you are a novice WCF developer, simply start from here:
http://blah.winsmarts.com/2008-4-Writing_the_WCF_Hello_World_App.aspx.

Custom Data Provider Class (Listing 4-6):

Before beginning, it is important to understand some of the key concepts. First, prepare to query data from those data sources that are not natively supported. Second, these operations must be asynchronous in order to perform the tasks in a timely fashion. And, most importantly, methods used must be thread-safe.

The Microsoft.Office.Visio.Server assembly provides these functionalities with its abstract class AddonDataHandler and its abstract methods that deal with all the necessary data module implementations.

Add a reference to Microsoft.Office.Visio.Server as the derived class will be inheriting the AddonDataHandler abstract class. It needs to also inherit the IAsyncResult interface from the System namespace to get the result of the asynchronous operation. Although there are many methods to override, the most important to understand are BeginGetData and EndGetData.

Visio Services calls the custom data provider's BeginGetData() method as soon as the request begins. Under the BeginData() method, create a thread and delegate a method to it. Create a callback method to be aware of when the thread completes its job:

```
ThreadPool.QueueUserWorkItem(new WaitCallback(GetData), callback);
```

In the GetData() method, create an instance to the WCF service object and call the GetServerStatusDetails method to retrieve the Server Status details:

```
ServerStatusClient oServerStatus = new ServerStatusClient();
DataTable dt = oServerStatus.GetServerStatusDetails();
this.Data.Reset();
this.Data.Tables.Add(dt);
this.Data.AcceptChanges();
```

After the set operation completes its job by retrieving the data, Visio Services calls the EndGetData() and returns the Data object as DataSet:

```
return this.Data;
```

VBA Code (Listing 4-8):

The VBA code is used to create and populate a data source that can be used by the Visio diagrams. This is similar to creating a data source using macros.

The code is very simple. It begins by initializing the data objects such as recordset, connection strings, command text, and so on:

```
Dim diagramServices As Integer
Dim vsoDataRecordset As Visio.dataRecordset
Dim dataRecordset As Visio.dataRecordset
Dim connectionString As String
Dim commandText As String
```

First, get to the instance of the diagram services of the active document, which is the page. Set the Visio Services version and the visibility of the external data sources window to true:

```
diagramServices = ActiveDocument.DiagramServicesEnabled
ActiveDocument.DiagramServicesEnabled = visServiceVersion140
Application.ActiveWindow.Windows.ItemFromID(visWinIDExternalData).Visible =
True
```

The following steps are optional here. They are to populate the external data source with values to facilitate if designer wants to bind the row data to the shapes in design mode. Connect to the SQL store, retrieve the record set, and add the record set to the active document data record set collection:

```
commandText = "SELECT ServerName, ServerIP, ServerStatus FROM
tblServerStatus"
connectionString = "Provider=SQLOLEDB;Data Source=<YourDataSourceName>;Initi
al Catalog=VisioServices;Integrated Security=SSPI; "
Set vsoDataRecordset = ActiveDocument.DataRecordsets.Add(connectionString,
commandText, 0, "Server Status Details")
```

Set the custom data provider assembly details to the recordset command string. Set and enable the diagram services to the active document:

```
vsoDataRecordset.DataConnection.connectionString = "DataModule=Altsis.VisioD
ataService,VisioDataService;"
ActiveDocument.DiagramServicesEnabled = diagramServices
```

So far, you've seen a lot of information on Visio and Visio Services. Now it's time to get to know some more references and information. You have seen the administration of Visio services using the UI in Central Administration. Now, you will learn more options for administering Visio Services using both CA and Windows PowerShell.

Summary

In this chapter, you learned about integrating Visio diagrams with SharePoint, configuration, and connecting to various data sources such as SQL Server or a SharePoint list.

What's Next?

In the next chapter, you will learn about administration of Visio services in SharePoint 2013 using UI and PowerShell.

CHAPTER 5

Administration of Visio Services

This chapter covers common adminstrative tasks for Visio. Commands for both Central Administration (CA) and PowerShell (PS) are included. We will also look at some of the factors affecting the performance of Visio Services. Note that these tasks apply to the on premises version of SharePoint. You have much less flexibility in Office 365.

Administering Visio Services can be done using either Central Administration (CA) or PowerShell (PS).

Tip To access PowerShell, simply click on Start ➤ All programs ➤ Microsoft SharePoint 2010 Products ➤ SharePoint 2013 Management Shell.

Best Practice:

1. Set up an application pool and a managed account before you begin. Most of the settings and configurations require both application pool accounts and managed accounts and you really don't want to go back to create them in the middle of operation. Plan ahead and make a list of all these accounts before you begin setting up your farm/application.

2. Make sure that you are member of the Administrators group. Again, you definitely need to be the local administrator for many obvious reasons. You don't want to start your application with a low privilege account and get access denied for an administration job.

Create a New Visio Graphics Service Application

From CA: from Application Management ➤ Manage Service Applications, click New and choose Visio Graphics Service. Provide the application name, choose application pool or create a new one, and choose or not to create an application proxy (add to default group) and click OK.

Using PS: at the PS prompt, type:

```
New-SPVisioServiceApplication <ServiceApplicationName> -
serviceapplicationpool <ServiceApplicationPoolName> -AddToDefaultGroup
```

Delete an Existing Visio Graphics Service Application

From CA: from Application Management ➤ Manage Service Applications, choose the Visio Graphics Service application name, then click on the Delete button on the ribbon.

Using PS: at the PS prompt, type:

```
Remove-SPServiceApplication <VisioServiceApplicationName>
```

List All Existing Visio Graphics Service Applications

From CA: from Application Management ➤ Click on Manage Service Applications to view all Visio Services Service applications.

Using PS: at the PS prompt, type:

```
Get-SPVisioServiceApplication
```

Creating a New Visio Graphics Service Application Proxy

From CA: You can only create an application proxy when creating a new Service application.

Using PS: at the PS prompt, type:

```
New-SPVisioServiceApplicationProxy <ServiceApplicationName>
```

▓ **Note** Service application proxies stand as the gateway or channel for connecting with service applications. They are deployed along with the service applications and encapsulate the components used to execute the calls on the service application.

Delete an Existing Visio Graphics Service Application Proxy

From CA: from Application Management ➤ Manage Service Applications, from the available Visio Service Proxies select the proxy from the list and Click Delete button from the ribbon.

Using PS: at the PS prompt, type:

```
Remove-SPServiceApplicationProxy <ProxyID>
```

List All Existing Visio Graphics Service Application Proxies

From CA: from Application Management ➤ Click on Manage Service Applications to view all available Visio Service Application Proxies under the selected Service Application.

Using PS: at the PS prompt, type:

```
Get-SPVisioServiceApplicationProxy
```

Set Up Visio Graphics Service Global Settings

From CA: from Application Management ➤ Manage Service Application, choose Visio Graphics Service ➤ Global Settings. You can now set Maximum Diagram Size, Minimum Cache Age, Maximum Cache Age, Maximum Recalc Duration, External Data.

Using PS: to set the performance parameters, at the PS prompt, type:

```
Set-SPVisioPeformance –MaxDiagramCacheAge <InMinutes> -MaxDiagramSize
<SizeInMB> -MaxRecalcDuration <InSeconds> -MinDiagramCacheAge
<InMinutes> - VisioServiceApplication <VisioServiceApplicationName>
```

To set the data configuration, at the PS prompt, type:

```
Set-SPVisioExternalData –VisioServiceApplication
<VisioServiceApplicationName> -UnattendedServiceAccountApplicationID
<ApplicationID>
```

Set Up a Graphics Service Trusted Data Provider

From CA: from Application Management ➤ Manage Service Application, choose Visio Graphics Service ➤ Trusted Data Providers. Now add a new, edit, or delete a Trusted Data Provider (for the how-to, refer to the SSS Section of this chapter).

Using PS: to create a new Trusted Data Provider, at the PS prompt, type:

```
New-SPVisioSafeDataProvider -DataProviderId <ProviderID>
-DataProviderType <Int32> -VIsioServiceApplication <VisioServiceApplication>
```

Using PS: to edit an existing Trusted Data Provider, at the PS prompt, type:

```
Set-SPVisioSafeDataProvider -DataProviderId <ProviderId>
-DataProviderType <Int32> -Description <String> -VisioServiceApplication
<VisioServiceAPplicationName>
```

Using PS: to delete an existing Trusted Data Provider, at the PS prompt, type:

```
Remove-SPVisioSafeDataProvider -DataProviderId <ProviderId>
-DataProviderType <Int32> -VisioServiceApplication
<VisioServiceApplicationName>
```

Factors Affecting Performance

Many factors are involved in the performance of the Visio Services. One of the key factors is often the infrastructure itself. If the following items don't help you to achieve optimum performance, keep in mind that the weak link may well be your infrastructure:

- Complexity of the drawing. This involves the number of shapes, data sources, and pages used, and so forth.

- Number of users accessing the drawing. The number of end users accessing a drawing simultaneously, especially during peak load hours, affect performance.

- Size of the drawing. The size of the drawing itself can be a factor; the more complex the drawing, the greater the size and this takes more time to render.

- Data source performance. External data sources connectivity, access, and performance all influence performance.

- Data refresh settings. As discussed earlier, when you have a smaller data refresh interval, you get more real-time access and less from the cache, which can hit performance badly.

■ **Note** For more information, please read the TechNet article "Plan Visio Services deployment" at http://technet.microsoft.com/en-us/library/ff356849.aspx.

Summary

In this chapter, you have learned about administration of Visio services in SharePoint 2013 using UI and Powershell.

What's New in Visio Services 2013

This appendix provides a useful overview of features that are new or changed in the current version of Visio Services—Visio Services 2013—for those who are familiar with Visio Services 2010.

Compatibility

Visio Services 2013 can render diagrams created both in Visio 2010 as well as Visio 2013. The major difference is the file format. Visio Services 2010 needed a specific file format called visio drawing file (.vdw) to render data-driven diagrams on SharePoint 2010 platform. The standard drawing file was .vdx then. However, Visio 2013 files will be saved now as .vsdx file and this one file will support natively what two files did in the last version. One important note with the new file format is that it does not support macros. In Chapter 4, you saved the file in .vdx format rather than vsdx for this very same reason; it does not support macros. In Visio 2013, the new file format to save the files that have macros is the new 'visio macro-enabled drawing' (.vsdm).

This feature is available in both on-premise and SharePoint Online versions.

Commenting

Visio Services 2013 now supports comment on the document. This enables users to collaborate on a single diagram and share and exchange comments, as shown in Figure A-1. Notice that this feature will not be available for diagrams created in Visio 2010 client.

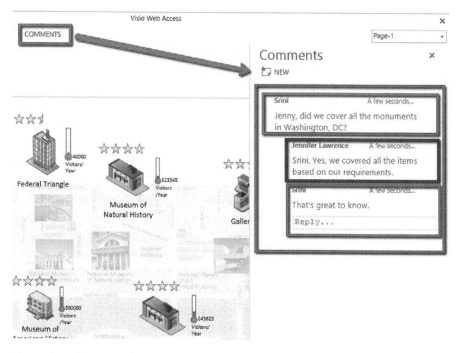

Figure A-1. *Comments feature in Visio Services*

This feature is available in both on-premise and SharePoint Online versions.

Rendering

Along with the introduction of new file formats mentioned earlier (.vsdx, .vsdm), the rendering format has also changed in Visio Services. These new file formats will be displayed in raster format, whereas Visio 2010 drawing files will still use Silverlight.

This feature is available in both on-premise and SharePoint Online versions.

Business Connectivity Services Data

Visio Services 2013 supports connectivity to external lists that are created based on external content type using Business Connectivity Services (BCS) on both on-premise and SharePoint online versions. However, the following data sources are not supported in SharePoint Online:

- SQL

- SQL Azure

- OLEDC

- ODBC

- custom data providers

In order to verify how to use Visio with BCS external list, let's perform an exercise. However, instead of using the on-premise version, you will use the SharePoint Online version.

PROBLEM CASE

Using database in SQL Azure, link data to Visio shapes by connecting with external list that is created based on external content type in BCS.

In order to achieve the required use case, you need to have the following:

- Office 365 subscription to host SharePoint Online Site

- SQL Azure Database

If you do not have these, I recommend that you at least obtain trial versions of those to try this exercise.

In a nutshell, you will be achieving what Figure A-2 depicts by the end of this exercise.

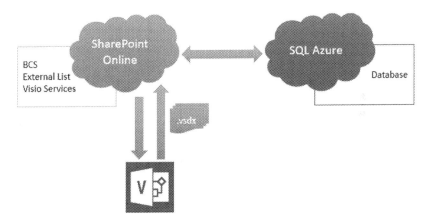

Figure A-2. *BCS exercise high-level design model*

1. In SQL Azure database, create a table with the following columns and name the table 'EmployeeBudgetInfo,' as shown in Table A-1 and Figure A-3.

Table A-1. *SQL Azure database design*

Column	Data Type
ID	Int
Employee Name	Nvarchar (100)
Year	Int
Budget	Money
Spent	Money
Email Address	Nvarchar (250)
Profile	Nvarchar (250)

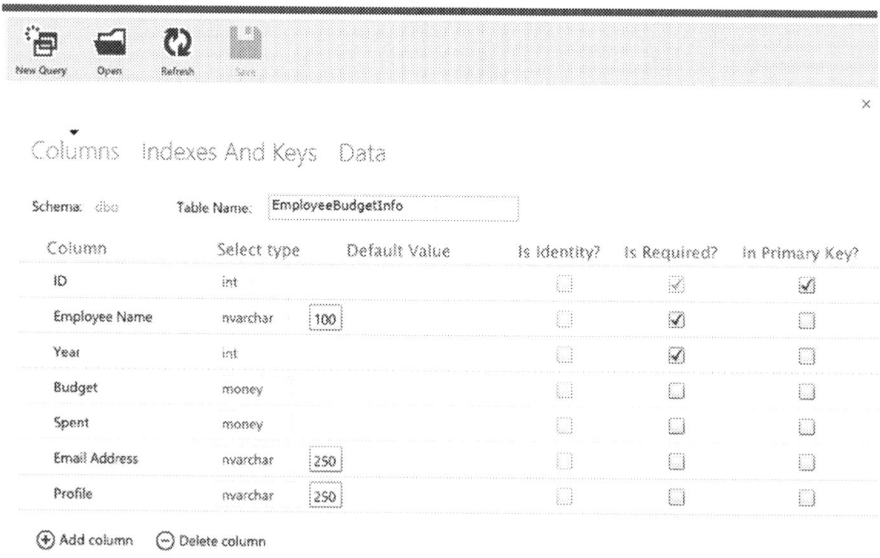

Figure A-3. *SQL Azure database table columns*

2. Open the SharePoint Online Admin site and click on Secure Store link, as shown in Figure A-4. Enter Target Application Settings, Application ID, Display Name, Contact Email, and Target Application Type. Leave the credential fields to default and enter the target application administrator.

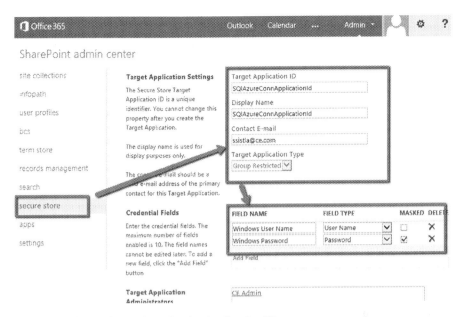

Figure A-4. *Set up Secure Store Service Application ID*

3. Once the target application ID is created, select and click on Set credentials, as shown in Figure A-5.

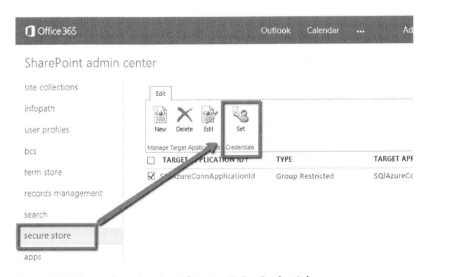

Figure A-5. *Secure Store Service Aplication ID Set Credentials*

4.   Set credentials for the secure store target application. In this case, the Windows user name will be the azure account that has access to the database. The password field is related to the account that you are going to use, as shown in Figure A-6.

set credentials for secure store target application (gr...

Target Application Name:	SQlAzureConnApplicationId
Target Application ID:	SQlAzureConnApplicationId
Credential Owners:	CE Admin

NAME	VALUE
Windows User Name	
Windows Password	
Confirm Windows Password	

Note: Once the credentials are set, they cannot be retrieved by the administrator. Any existing credentials for this credential owner will be overwritten.

OK   Cancel

Figure A-6. *Secure Store Service Application Set User Name, Password*

5.   While you are in the admin window, click on the 'bcs' link on the left navigation and select the option 'Manage BDC Models and External Content Types,' as shown in Figure A-7.

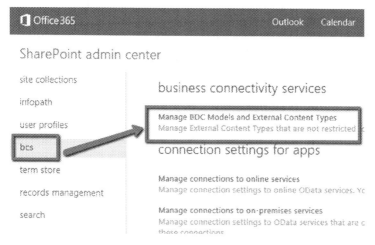

Figure A-7. *Mange BDC Models and External Content Types for BCS in SharePoint Online*

6. Click on 'Set Metadata Store Permissions' on the Permissions section of the Edit tab, as shown in Figure A-8.

Figure A-8. *Set BCS Metdata Store Permissions*

7. Under the set metadata store permissions window, add account information that has access to SQL Azure database and provide all of the permissions and click the OK button, as shown in Figure A-9.

set metadata store permissions

To add an account, or group, type or select it below and click 'Add'.

| | Add |

To remove an account, or group, select it above and click 'Remove'. | Remove |

Permissions

☐ Propagate permissions to all BDC Models, External Systems and External Content Types in the BDC Metadata Store. Doing so will overwrite existing permissions.

Figure A-9. *Set Permissions to BCS metadata store*

8. Open SharePoint Designer and launch the SharePoint online site. Select External Content Types and click on 'External Content Type' from the ribbon.

9. In the new 'External Content Type' window, enter values for 'Name,' 'Display Name,' and click on the 'External System' link: 'Click here to discover external data sources and define operations.'

10. Under the 'Operations Designer,' click the 'Add Connection' button.

11. Choose 'SQL Server' from the available data source types and click the OK button.

12. Under the 'SQL Server Connection' window, enter the Azure SQL database server information and Database Name.

13. Choose the 'Connect with Impersonated Custom Identity' option and enter the ApplicationID you created earlier in this exercise. Click on the OK button, as shown in Figure A-10.

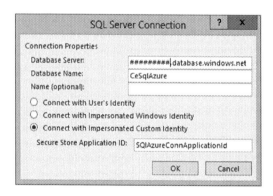

Figure A-10. *Configure SQL Server Connection*

14. The action performed in the last step should connect to your Azure SQL database provided that the credentials that you set in the secure store services are accurate.

15. Under the 'Data Source Explorer' expand Tables, right-click on the table that you created in SQL Azure and choose 'Create All Operations,' as shown in Figure A-11.

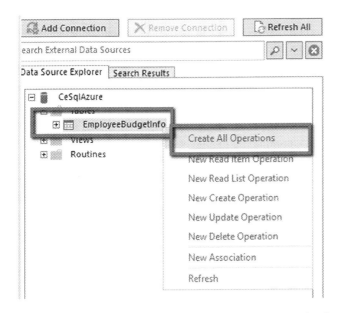

Figure A-11. *Creating CRUD operations on the SQL Azure database table*

16. Once all of the operations are created successfully, save the external content type.

17. You have two options at this stage: you can create an external list from SharePoint Designer by selecting the ECT that you just created or you can use SharePoint to sit and create an external list. In this exercise, we will use the SharePoint site option.

18. Close SharePoint Designer and open your SharePoint Site.

19. From the site gear icon, choose Add an app and select 'External List.'

20. Under the 'Adding External List' window, pick a name, and from the 'External Content Type,' choose the one that you created earlier, as shown in Figure A-12.

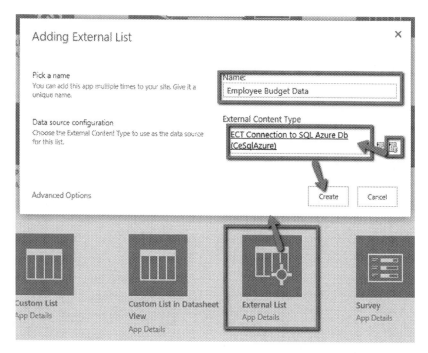

Figure A-12. *Adding an External List*

21. Once an external list is created, add new items using the new item creation window accessed from the ribbon, as shown in Figure A-13.

ID *	
Employee Name *	
Year *	
Budget	
Spent	
Email Address	
Profile	

Save   Cancel

Figure A-13. *New item entry form*

22. Create new items based on Figure A-14.

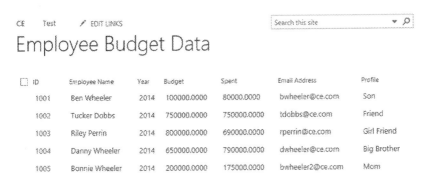

Figure A-14. SharePoint External List with data

23. Launch Visio 2013 and create a drawing file with Organization Chart template.

24. If you choose blank drawing, you can select the shapes from More Shapes ➤ Business ➤ Organization Chat and select 'Belt - Organization Chart Shapes,' as shown in Figure A-15.

Figure A-15. Choosing stencil in Visio 2013

25. Add Executive Belt and Manager Belt shapes to the drawing.

26. Using Define Shape Data, add Label as 'Name,' and set values to shape that match to the Employee Name, as shown in Figure A-16.

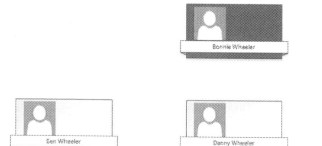

Figure A-16. *Add shapes to the Visio diagram*

27. From the Data tab, click on Link Data to Shapes and choose the Microsoft SharePoint Foundation list option. Click Next, as shown in Figure A-17.

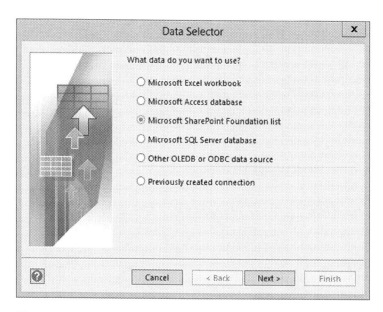

Figure A-17. *Data Selector window*

28. Choose the External List that you created in earlier steps and select the radio button 'Link to a list.' Click Next, as shown in Figure A-18.

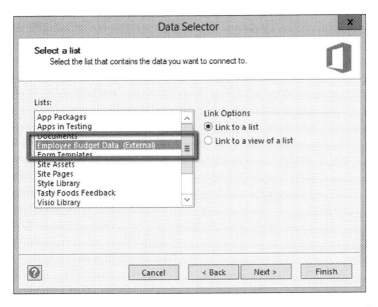

Figure A-18. *Choosing SharePoint External List in the Data Selector window*

29. External Data tab will display the data that exists in the external list, as shown in Figure A-19.

ID	Employee Name	Year	Budget	Spent	Email Address	Profile
1001	Ben Wheeler	2014	100000.0000	80000.0000	bwheeler@ce.com	Project Manager
1002	Tucker Dobbs	2014	750000.0000	750000.0000	tdobbs@ce.com	Project Manager
1003	Riley Perrin	2014	800000.0000	690000.0000	rperrin@ce.com	Software Developer
1004	Danny Wheeler	2014	650000.0000	790000.0000	dwheeler@ce.com	Project Manager
1005	Bonnie Wheeler	2014	200000.0000	175000.0000	bwheeler2@ce.com	Program Manager

Figure A-19. *External Data window in Visio 2013*

30. Right-click on one of the shapes and select the option 'Edit data graphics.'

31. Click on 'New Item...' and, from the Data field, select the 'More Fields...' option, as shown in Figure A-20.

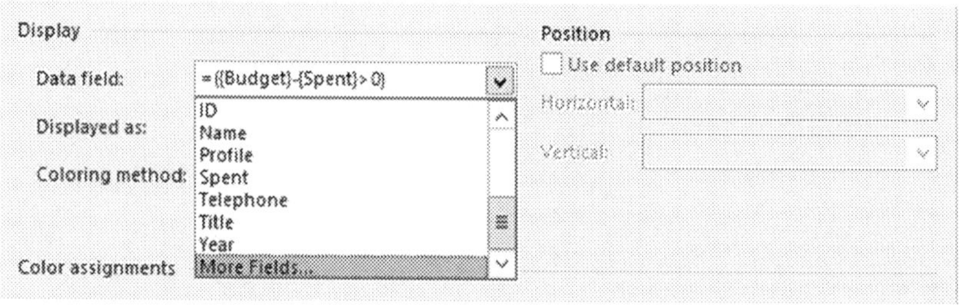

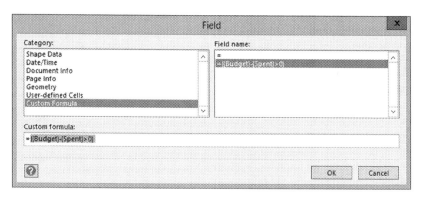

Figure A-20. *Choosing custom fields*

Under the Field window, select Custom Formula and type the following in the Custom formula: input, as shown in Figure A-21. Click OK:

```
=({Budget}-{Spent} >0)
```

Figure A-21. *Creating custom formulas for custom fields*

32. Choose Displayed as value to be 'Color by Value.'

33. Choose Coloring method value to be 'Each color represents a unique value.'

34. For values 0, 1 set fill colors, as shown in Figure A-22.

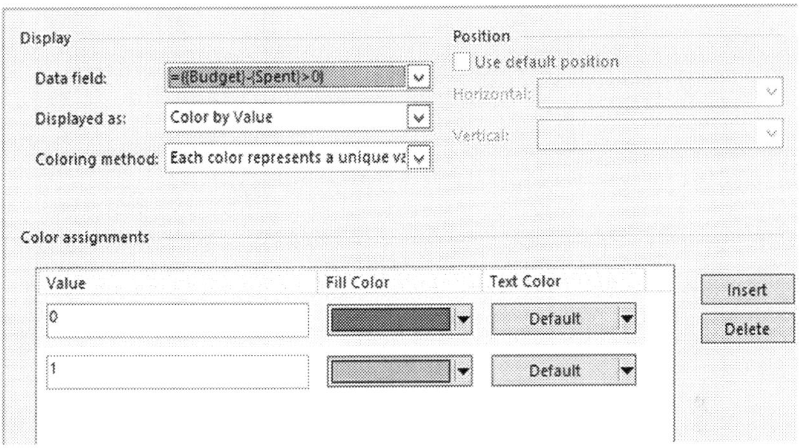

Figure A-22. *Choosing data graphic options*

35. Create another new item and select custom formula field as in the previous step. Set the formula:

   ={Budget}-{Spent}

36. Use Icon Set as Displayed as the value and choose flags Style.

37. Set values less than 0 to show a red flag and values greater than or equal to 0 as green, and click OK.

38. Create another New item, and choose the Profile column as the Data field.

39. Choose Text value for the Displayed as option and select Heading 1 as Style.

40. Create another new item and select the custom formula field. Set the formula:

```
=({Spent}/{Budget})*100
```

41. Choose Data Bar value for the Displayed as option.

42. Choose 'Progress circle' as style.

43. Remove the Value Format and Label options and click OK.

44. Your final data graphics window should look like Figure A-23.

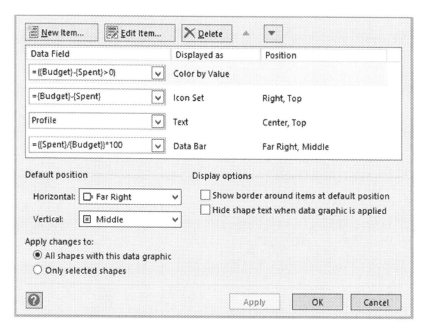

Figure A-23. *Data graphics*

45. From the External Data window, drag and drop the row data that matches the 'Name' shape data value.

46. This action should apply the data graphics created in earlier steps to the selected shape, as shown in Figure A-24.

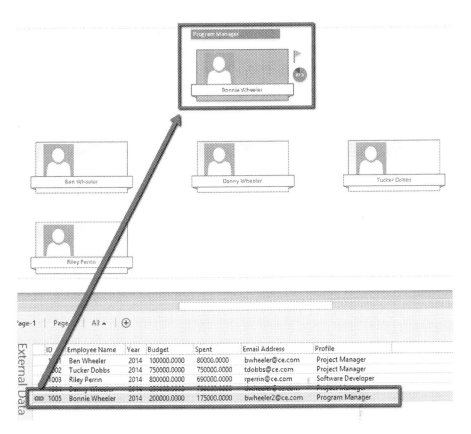

Figure A-24. Linking data to shape

47. From the Data tab, External Data section, click on the Automatically Link button.

48. Under the 'Automatic Link -' window, choose the 'All shapes on this page' option and click 'Next.'

49. Choose the Data Column as 'Employee Name,' select 'Shape Field' as 'Name,' and click 'Next,' as shown in Figure A-25.

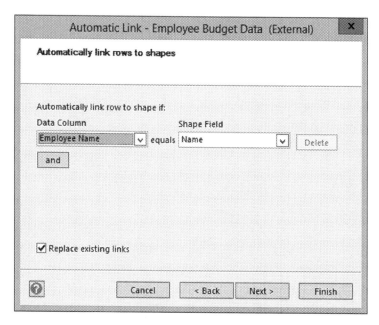

Figure A-25. *Automatically link rows to shapes*

50. Click on 'Finish' to automatically link rows to shapes using your selected criteria.

51. Your Visio diagram should look like Figure A-26.

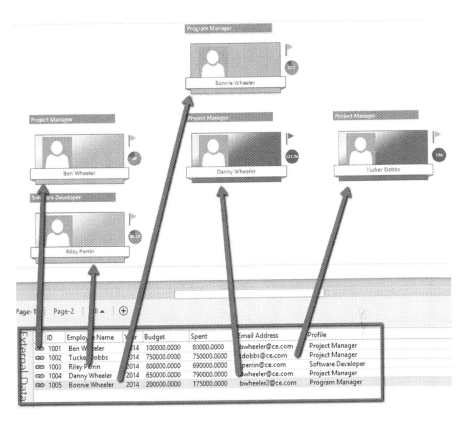

Figure A-26. *Automatically link rows to shapes*

52. Save the Visio drawing file to your SharePoint Online site in the Visio document library. Create one if you have not created the library yet.

53. Alternatively, you can choose to save the file to your local file system and upload it to the SharePoint site.

54. Launch your SharePoint Online site and access the document library where you saved the Visio drawing file.

55. Click on the drawing file to open it in the browser displaying the shape data, as shown in Figure A-27.

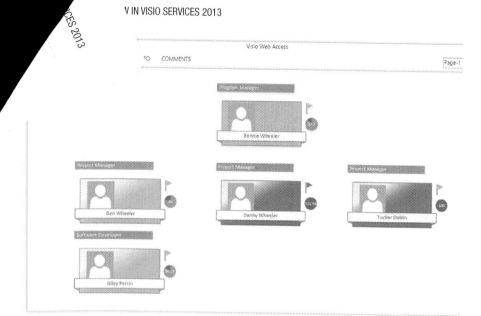

Figure A-27. *Visio Diagram in SharePoint 2013 with BCS external list data*

56. Change values in the external list and the shape data
information will change accordingly.

Index

■ W, X, Y, Z

Get the eBook for only $10!

Now you can take the weightless companion with you anywhere, anytime. Your purchase of this book entitles you to 3 electronic versions for only $10.

This Apress title will prove so indispensible that you'll want to carry it with you everywhere, which is why we are offering the eBook in 3 formats for only $10 if you have already purchased the print book.

Convenient and fully searchable, the PDF version enables you to easily find and copy code—or perform examples by quickly toggling between instructions and applications. The MOBI format is ideal for your Kindle, while the ePUB can be utilized on a variety of mobile devices.

Go to www.apress.com/promo/tendollars to purchase your companion eBook.